Independent Reading:
Creating
Lifelong Readers

Previously published as *Creating Lifelong Readers Through Independent Reading*

Barbara Moss & Terrell A. Young

SCHOLASTIC INC.

Executive Editor, Books   Corinne M. Mooney
Developmental Editor   Charlene M. Nichols
Developmental Editor   Tori Mello Bachman
Developmental Editor   Stacey L. Reid
Editorial Production Manager   Shannon T. Fortner
Design and Composition Manager   Anette Schuetz

Project Editors   Tori Mello Bachman and Wesley Ford

Cover   Design, Lise Holliker Dykes; Photographs, © iStockphoto.com/nano (third from top), © Shutterstock Images LLC (all others)

Previously published as *Creating Lifelong Readers Through Independent Reading*

ISBN 978-0-545-86949-2

12 11 10 9 8 7 6 5 4 3 2 1   15 16 17 18 19 20/0

Printed in the U.S.A.   23

First Scholastic printing, April 2015

We dedicate this book to all of the teachers who love reading and books and who work so hard to pass this love on to their students

—B.M. and T.Y.

CONTENTS

 **Barbara Moss** is a university professor at San Diego State University. She has been a professor of literacy education for more than 20 years. She presently teaches courses in content area literacy and children's literature at the credential and master's levels. Before moving into higher education, Barbara was a middle and high school reading and language arts teacher and a K–8 reading supervisor. She has also worked as a literacy coach in an urban San Diego High School.

She is the author and editor of numerous journal articles; her work has appeared in *The Reading Teacher,* the *Journal of Literacy Research,* and the *Reading and Writing Quarterly.* She has also published numerous books related to close reading, children's literature, and teacher development. Her research interests focus on the uses of informational texts in classroom, content area literacy, and teacher development.

Barbara has served as a professional developer for schools across the United States. She has given hundreds of professional presentations at conferences and online. She can be reached at bmoss@mail.sdsu.edu.

 **Terrell A. Young**, professor of children's literature at Brigham Young University, is serving as a member of the Board of Directors of the United States Board on Books for Young People (USBBY). He was president of the Washington Organization for Reading Development, the Washington State International Literacy Association affiliate, from 2000–2001; Terry also served as president of the ILA Children's Literature and Reading Special Interest Group from 2004–2006 and the National Council of Teachers of English Children's Literature Assembly from 2006–2008. From 2009–2012 he served on the ILA Board of Directors. Terry has been a member of many children's book award committees and was honored with the ILA's Outstanding Teacher Education in Reading Award in 2006.

Terry's scholarly interests include children's literature, literature-based practices, and the creative processes of authors and illustrators. His articles have appeared in many venues, including *Bookbird, Book Links, Childhood Education, Language Arts,* and *The Reading Teacher.* He coauthored or edited a number of books, including *Children's Literature, Briefly* (with Michael Tunnell, James Jacobs, & Gregory Bryan), and *Children's Literature and the Common Core State Standards* (with Rachel Wadham).

Terry and his wife, Christine, are the parents of four adult children—Jonathan, Natalie, Emilee, and Jeffrey. He can be reached at terrell_young@byu.edu.

PREFACE

The goal of *Creating Lifelong Readers Through Independent Reading* is to provide classroom teachers and librarians with a plethora of strategies for making independent reading a part of every classroom. The idea for this book sprang from our deep love of literature. We both believe in books and their power to make literacy learning and teaching both meaningful and magical. This book stems from our deep and abiding concern that texts matter in classrooms; we believe that students need books and books need readers. In a time when reading is being marginalized and replaced with scripted reading programs, we want to reestablish the importance of independent reading to the curriculum. Most important, we want to offer concrete suggestions about how to create independent reading programs that make a difference.

As Dorris (2006) states,

> Great books, whenever in our lives we encounter them, expand our humanity; forge links with other people, past, present, and future; open our eyes; allow us the perspective of a wider view. A book is the emissary from the world to a single person, and the act of reading is, at heart, a quiet, but mighty dialogue. (p. 590)

We hope that by engaging students with independent reading they become participants in the "quiet, but mighty dialogue" that can only exist between a text and a reader. Through this dialogue, students can find themselves, explore the world, and discover the lifelong pleasure that reading can provide.

Each of the chapters in this book is designed to provide classroom-tested ideas for creating independent reading programs. Chapter 1 establishes a foundation, providing a thorough introduction to independent reading and a rationale for its use. In addition, it provides essential research-based evidence for the efficacy of independent reading.

Chapter 2 explores ways in which you, the classroom teacher, can make the classroom library the centerpiece for the independent reading program. It provides suggestions for organizing the space, making books accessible to students, and organizing the book collection. In addition, it offers recommendations for the kinds of books every classroom library needs. Finally, it provides suggestions for matching readers with books that motivate them—a critical aspect of any independent reading program.

Chapter 3 provides you with ways to successfully create structures that support independent reading. It provides information on time schedules, record keeping, conferencing, and accountability. Special emphasis is placed on ways to get maximum benefit from student–teacher conferencing. In addition, this chapter introduces a variety of forms useful for maintaining student records.

Chapter 4 demonstrates how you can link strategic literacy instruction with independent reading. It provides a plethora of ideas for promoting responses to literature and informational texts through activities that include journal writing, creative dramatics and artistic responses, and wiki creation.

Chapter 5 suggests ways that you can make independent reading a part of content area instruction. This chapter demonstrates how independent reading can contribute to the development of content-related background knowledge through student reading of nonfiction and informational texts. It also provides suggestions for selecting books in the content area classroom and ways to motivate student interest in content area learning through trade books. This chapter provides sample focus lessons and suggestions for student–teacher conferences about nonnarrative texts.

Four additional noteworthy features of our text deserve mention here. First, we want to point out the interviews with notable reading experts that appear at the end of each chapter. These interviews provide insights from scholars whose work has shaped the field of literacy in general and our thinking about independent reading in particular. Second, because we know how busy our fellow teachers are, Appendix A contains a number of handy reproducibles you can use in the classroom to structure your own independent reading program. Third, because we are keenly aware of the important role that parents play in helping their children become readers, you will find in Appendix B reproducibles of simple, practical tip sheets you can hand out to parents to promote independent reading in the home. Finally, the literature cited list provides a quick guide to every children's book referenced in the text, which can be a valuable resource for teachers and children of all ages.

In conclusion, we would like to thank the peer reviewers—James Phillips, Howard Miller, Angela Salmon, Ambika Gopalakrishnan, and Phyllis Wilkinson—whose thoughtful comments helped us hone this book. We also wish to thank the literacy scholars we interviewed for generously sharing their time and expertise with us—Richard L. Allington, Tony Stead, Linda B. Gambrell, Sharon Taberski, and Myra Zarnowski. This book is much stronger because of their contributions. We also wish to acknowledge our family members and former teachers who shared their love of literature and reading with us. By sharing their time and their passion for stories, literature, and reading, they have made our lives much richer, and we continue to benefit from their magical endowments.

CHAPTER 1

Making the Case and a Place for Independent Reading

Reading is powerful. It creates compassion, moves us to action, transports us to different places, and even sometimes transforms us. Reading can change lives.

Of all the goals for literacy instruction, there is none more critical than creating students who read independently. Independent reading provides practice and pleasure and a passion for books. It affords the opportunity to get lost in a book—to be so engaged in reading that we lose track of time, of place, of everything but the power of a text to transport and change us. Repeated experiences that involve true engagement with books help students develop a love of reading that may last a lifetime.

Independent reading is a hot topic—just look at the book club phenomenon: Book clubs have been springing up all over the world. It is estimated that there are more than 100,000 book clubs in the United States alone (Daniels, 2002). Book clubs cater to readers of different tastes; some focus on football, mystery stories, antiques, or artists. There are book clubs for prisoners, for African American women, for doctors and lawyers, and for political radicals. When Oprah Winfrey recommends books for her book club on television, sales of those titles skyrocket. Entire communities have gotten in on the act; citywide "One City, One Book" reading programs are thriving in major cities such as San Francisco and Chicago. Oakland, California, for example, recently encouraged residents to read *The Mistress of Spices* (Divakaruni, 1997), a best-selling book set in that city. Book discussion groups sprang up all over Oakland while other groups met online. Likewise, universities are getting into the action. For instance, McCarthy's (2002) *Lay That Trumpet in Our Hands* was assigned reading for all of Michigan State University's incoming freshman students as part of the East Lansing and Michigan State University One Book, One Community reading program. During orientation week, students had the opportunity to discuss the book in small groups and participate in a range of activities related to the book. While not all avid readers are members of book clubs, all share the profound pleasure that reading can bring.

Unfortunately, however, book club participation is not the norm; far more people in the United States choose not to read. Similarly, many students at all levels choose not to read. If international comparisons are to be believed, interest in reading outside of school is limited even in the early grades, declines in the middle grades, and continues its descent through the high school years. According to Noyes (2000),

> Aliteracy seems to reinforce itself. Children who do not read do not develop their reading skills. Children, like most of us, dislike doing things they do poorly, so they tend to read less and less…. Aliteracy is potentially as alarming as illiteracy. Educators need to look at factors such as their attitude toward children, the way children learn, and the curriculum. These factors may have an enormous impact on creating lifelong positive attitudes about reading. (pp. 313–314)

The 2001 Progress in International Reading Literacy Study (PIRLS), an assessment of reading comprehension and reading habits of fourth graders in 35 countries (including the United States), found the following trends:

- Only 35% of U.S. fourth graders reported reading for fun daily.
- An average of 40% of fourth graders internationally read for fun daily.
- Thirty-two percent of U.S. fourth graders reported *never* reading for fun outside of school.
- An average of 18% of international fourth graders never read for fun outside of school.

These statistics are disappointing, although they may help explain why U.S. student scores on international assessments are not as high as we would like. Interestingly, those U.S. fourth graders who read for fun every day had higher average scores on the PIRLS assessment compared with those who never or almost never read for fun. This pattern holds at the international level as well, based on international averages (National Center for Education Statistics, 2001).

Independent reading is just one component of a quality reading program, but it is a critical one—not a substitute for direct instruction in basic reading skills, but a critical support for students learning to read, as well as reading to learn. Furthermore, its implementation need not be delayed until students master basic reading skills but rather should be provided as a powerful accompaniment to skills instruction. Independent reading ensures that students get rich opportunities to apply the skills that they learn during shared reading, guided reading, and other literacy-related experiences. According to Pearson (2005), "all the explicit instruction in the world will not make strong readers unless accompanied by lots of experience applying their knowledge, skills, and strategies during actual reading" (p. 6).

An effective reading program is more than just a basal reader program. It incorporates independent reading experiences that engage students in reading beyond the basal. As Allington (2006) notes, "No basal reading series contains enough reading material to develop high levels of reading proficiency in children.... The same is true of social studies and science textbooks" (p. 49). He points out that greater volume of reading is a distinguishing feature of high-achieving classrooms and recommends that students read independently in school for 90 minutes or more each day.

Independent reading provides the reinforcement that all students need to become the best readers they can be. This practice builds fluency, improves comprehension, increases vocabulary, and creates confidence in young readers. As Cunningham and Stanovich (1998) state,

> A child who reads abundantly develops greater reading skills, a larger vocabulary, and more general knowledge about the world. In return [the child has] increased reading comprehension and, therefore, enjoys more pleasurable reading experiences and is encouraged to read even more. (p. 65)

This Matthew effect, a term based on a Biblical reference, results in a situation where the more students read, the better readers they become. The more skilled they are at reading, the more likely they are to embrace it.

The increased knowledge about the world that reading provides gives students a rich background for all kinds of learning and contributes to success on standardized tests. The student who develops a consuming interest in books about dinosaurs, for example, brings increased knowledge and understanding to a science unit on prehistoric times. Hirsch (2006) argues that this knowledge is even more crucial to academic success than students' abilities to use reading strategies like prediction, clarifying, summarization, and so on.

Without independent reading experiences, which are critical to the development of reading comprehension skills, vocabulary development, and background knowledge, students miss valuable opportunities for the sustained reading practice that can lead to fluency, develop confidence, and promote motivation for reading. Furthermore, students' reading is confined to a narrow range of materials, usually basal readers and content area textbooks, which typically do not reflect the interests of youngsters (Hanjian, 1985; Pieronek, 1985). Perhaps most important, students are denied the opportunity to engage with texts that they can choose for themselves about topics that matter to them.

Independent Reading: What It Is and What It Is Not

Independent reading, also called voluntary reading, self-selected reading, or leisure reading, is reading that students do on their own in or out of school, with or without accompanying instruction. It may be as simple as a student picking a book to read from the classroom library and taking it home, or it may involve more structured, teacher-directed experiences that incorporate instruction on how to select a book, matching students with books at their level, or monitoring student comprehension through conferences or other forms of accountability. Whenever or wherever students are reading on their own, without teacher assistance, they are reading independently.

Independent reading is a critical component of a quality reading program, but it cannot be the entire reading program. Independent reading provides an important complement to direct skills instruction, but it cannot be a substitute for such instruction. Independent reading creates an opportunity for practice of reading skills, but it is not superfluous to instruction. Independent reading provides rich opportunities for students to select their own books from a wide range of materials rather than being constrained by basal readers or content area textbooks.

Time for independent reading is not time wasted: Students should be accountable for this time in some way. Just as teachers focus student attention on "accountable talk," accountable independent reading time helps students recognize that, although time for reading can and should provide enjoyment, it represents a part of the school day that is meaningful and focused on a task. Table 1 presents a quick summary of what quality in-school independent reading is—and is not.

Recreational reading, one form of independent reading, is when students read books specifically chosen at their recreational reading level, which means that they can decode and comprehend most of the words in the text (Palumbo & Willcutt, 2007). Student independent reading experiences should provide opportunities to read a wide range of books, but a large percentage of these books should be at the recreational level. If students consistently read books that are too easy or too difficult for them, they will not benefit from the experience.

Independent reading is a critical piece of the puzzle that is reading instruction. It should not be implemented haphazardly; instead, like every aspect of reading instruction, it should be planned, structured, and made a part of students' daily literacy experiences. It is not solely the

Table 1. What Independent Reading Is and Is Not

What Independent Reading Is	What Independent Reading Is Not
• A critical component of a quality reading program	• A substitute for a quality reading program
• A powerful accompaniment to direct skills instruction	• A substitute for direct skills instruction
• An opportunity for students to practice reading skills	• An unnecessary add-on to instruction
• A chance for students to self-select a wide range of reading materials (trade books, magazines, newspapers, etc.) of interest to them	• Reading selections in the basal reader
• Class time during which students are on task and accountable for their reading	• Class time during which students are off task and unaccountable for their reading
• An organized systematic program that involves the classroom, the school, and the community	• A haphazard attempt to get students to read more
• A collaborative effort among teachers, students, administrators, parents, school and public librarians, and community members	• The sole responsibility of the teacher

responsibility of the teacher or the student but rather a collaborative effort among teachers, students, administrators, parents, school and public librarians, and community members.

Reluctant Independent Readers

Some states have requirements—an "opportunity to read" standard—for independent reading as part of the language arts curriculum. For example, the California language arts content standards require that students read 500,000 words outside of school by the end of fourth grade and one million words by the eighth grade (California Department of Education, 2008). The New York content standards require that students read 25 books annually (University of the State of New York and the State Education Department, n.d.). To achieve these goals, many schools require students to read at home for 10 minutes or more daily. To help with this, teachers often take students to the library, require that they locate a book, and then ask students to take the book home and read it every day.

Many students, however, hurriedly go through the motions of picking a book, any book, even one that may be inappropriate in level and of little interest to them. They take the book home, leaf through the pages, and, more often than not, either don't read the book at all or "pretend read" the book to complete the requisite minutes. Some, but not all, of these students are struggling readers. All could be characterized as reluctant independent readers. They aren't familiar with many book titles or authors, are not sure how to select books, and have no idea how to locate books of interest to them.

All too often, these students add independent reading to their long list of unsuccessful reading experiences. They associate reading with failure, tedium, and struggle. As a result, they don't get the practice they need, they don't find pleasure in reading, and they never become accomplished readers, let alone lifelong readers. These reluctant independent readers may actually *lose* academic ground because of their failure to read, even if they are not initially struggling readers (Mullis, Campbell, & Farstrup, 1993).

The Role of Teachers, Parents, and Librarians

Teachers, parents, and librarians can often prevent the previously described scenario by sharing intriguing trade book titles with students through read-alouds, book talks, book displays, and much more. You can provide access to a rich array of books on myriad topics. You can create classroom environments that engage students with books in ways that create communities of readers (Hepler & Hickman, 1982). You can teach students to find books that are appropriate to their ability levels, engage them, and keep them coming back for more. In addition, you can make students accountable for their reading in ways that don't extinguish enthusiasm for books.

To paraphrase Jacobs (Herrick & Jacobs, 1955), love of reading is caught—not taught. One of your most important responsibilities is to help students catch the desire to read. Some students achieve this on their own, but a great many do not. Virtually all students can benefit from the enthusiasm, interest, and expertise of an adult—teacher, parent, or librarian—who knows children's books. Heightening students' awareness of the exhilarating possibilities of print can acquaint them with the joy of literature and provide them with a love of reading that may last a lifetime.

Clearly this is most easily accomplished if you not only love books but also have in-depth knowledge of children's trade books. Even the best teachers, however, need school, parental, and community support if they are to achieve the goal of creating engaged independent readers. Parents who themselves read and have books in the home provide powerful reading models for their children. School and public librarians play critical roles in promoting the importance of reading for pleasure and can be potent allies in the effort to make books central in students' lives. Schoolwide and community independent reading efforts can also bolster your efforts to make books indispensable in students' lives.

Positive independent reading experiences that ensure success for every student are vital to the development of students who not only can read but also choose to read. Organized, systematic efforts to make independent reading central in the lives of students are essential. Such experiences can create students who want to continue reading after the bell has rung—students who "read like a wolf eats," as Paulsen (2007) describes the ravenous hunger for books that drives book lovers. Careful guidance, along with school and community support, can help students become successful, engaged independent readers who grow into book-loving adults.

What Can Research Tell Us About Independent Reading?

Much has been made of the failure of the National Reading Panel (NRP; National Institute of Child Health and Human Development [NICHD], 2000) to endorse programs designed to encourage independent reading. The NRP found that hundreds of correlational studies indicate that the more students read, the better their fluency, comprehension, and vocabulary. These studies do not prove that independent reading *causes* improved reading achievement, however. Because the NRP included only experimental studies in its report, it excluded these correlational studies in its analysis. It was unable to locate a sufficient number of experimental studies to either support or reject the use of independent reading as a means of increasing reading achievement. This is what the NRP concluded:

> There is still not sufficient research evidence obtained from studies of high methodological quality to support the idea that such efforts reliably increase how much students read or that such programs result in improved reading skills. Given the extensive use of these techniques, it is important that such research be conducted...these findings do not negate the positive influence that independent silent reading may have on reading fluency, nor do the findings negate the possibility that wide independent reading significantly influences vocabulary development and reading comprehension. Rather, there are simply not sufficient data from well-designed studies capable of testing questions of causation to substantiate causal claims. The available data do suggest that independent silent reading is not an effective practice when used as the *only type of reading instruction* [italics added] to develop fluency and other reading skills, particularly with students who have not yet developed critical alphabetic and word reading skills. (NICHD, 2000, p. 13)

The findings of the NRP did not confirm the assertion that time spent reading is definitely responsible for increased achievement. The report clearly stated, however, that independent silent reading is not effective when used as the *only type of literacy instruction*. In other words, a reading program that neglects instruction and simply focuses on independent reading is not likely to be successful. Independent reading should be *one component* of a balanced literacy program that includes a range of instructional activities focusing on decoding, fluency, vocabulary, comprehension development, and so on.

Numerous studies suggest that independent reading is associated with a number of academic, affective, school/classroom, and home benefits. The controversial findings of the NRP report (NICHD, 2000) regarding independent reading, however, have led to increased numbers of experimental studies on this topic. Since 2003, more researchers (Reutzel, Fawson, & Smith, 2008; Stahl & Heuback, 2005; Wu & Samuels, 2004) have begun to use experimental research methods to determine whether independent reading can, in fact, support gains in reading achievement. These studies support the use of independent reading instruction under specific conditions and are discussed in the sections that follow. New models of independent reading that inform practice and promote achievement are important to consider as more and more experimental research is conducted and those conditions that best support independent reading in schools, classrooms, and the home and community are discovered.

Benefits of Independent Reading

Wide independent reading is associated with a number of academic and affective benefits; however, in the sections that follow, we will focus specifically on these five outcomes:

1. Increased vocabulary development
2. Greater domain and background knowledge
3. Better fluency and comprehension
4. Improved reading achievement
5. Greater interest in books and motivation to read

We have reviewed selected studies associated with these outcomes, including classic studies related to independent reading as well as those studies of greatest interest to teachers, parents, and librarians. Many of these studies cannot *prove* whether independent reading causes increased achievement or whether it creates a more positive attitude about reading; however, they do tell us that a relationship between reading and these benefits does exist, as we explore in the next section. Taken together, this research provides compelling evidence for the value of independent reading. Table 2 and Table 3 provide references for these and other studies that support these findings.

Table 2. Studies on the Benefits of Independent Reading

Type of Factors	Benefits	Research Studies
Academic factors	Increased vocabulary development	• Cunningham & Stanovich, 1998 • Nagy & Anderson, 1984
	Greater domain and background knowledge	• Block & Mangieri, 1996 • Cunningham & Stanovich, 1991 • Guthrie & Greaney, 1991 • Ravitch & Finn, 1987 • Stanovich & Cunningham, 1993
	Better fluency and comprehension	• Allington, 2006 • Cunningham, 2005 • Elley & Mangubhai, 1983 • Kuhn, 2004 • Reutzel & Hollingsworth, 1991 • Reutzel, Fawson, & Smith 2008 • Samuels & Wu, 2003
	Improved reading achievement	• Anderson, Wilson, & Fielding, 1988 • Cullinan, 2000 • Cunningham & Stanovich, 1998 • Guthrie, 2002 • Guthrie, Anderson, Alao, & Rinehart, 1999 • Heyns, 1978 • Kim, 2003 • Krashen, 2004 • Kuhn, 2004 • Manning & Manning, 1984 • Taylor, Frye, & Maruyama, 1990 • Weisendanger, 1982
Affective factors	Greater interest in books and motivation to read	• Allington, 1994 • Asher & Markell, 1974 • Gambrell, Codling, & Palmer, 1996 • Guthrie & Greaney, 1991 • Schiefele, 1991 • Worthy, 1996 • Worthy, Moorman, & Turner, 1999 • Yoon, 2002

Table 3. Studies of the Factors That Contribute to Independent Reading Success

Type of Factors	Factor	Research Studies
Classroom and school factors	Classroom and school environments	• Blatt, 1981 • Hiebert, Mervar, & Person, 1990 • Mendoza, 1985 • Morrow, 1983
	Appealing classroom and school libraries	• Fractor, Woodruff, Martinez, & Teale, 1993 • Krashen, 1995 • Lance, Welborn, & Hamilton-Pennell, 1993 • McQuillan, 1998 • Morrow, 2003 • Neuman, 1999 • Sinclair-Tarr & Tarr, 2007
	Access to a range of books	• Guthrie, Schafer, Von Secker, & Alban, 2000 • Kiefer, 1988 • Kim, 2003 • Morrow, 1992 • Neuman & Celano, 2001
	Teachers who promote reading	• Applegate & Applegate, 2004 • Block & Mangieri, 2002 • Cameron & Pierce, 1995 • Morrison, Jacobs, & Swinyard, 1999
	Reading incentive programs	• Marinak & Gambrell, 2008
Home and community factors	Rich home literacy environments	• Durkin, 1966 • Morrow, 1983 • Tabors, Snow, & Dickinson, 2001 • Wasik, 2004
	Community-based partnerships that support reading	• Invernizzi, Rosemary, Juel, & Richards, 1997 • Rodriguez-Brown, Li, & Albon, 1999 • Segel & Friedberg, 1991
	Public libraries that support reading	• Association for Library Service to Children, 1996 • Morrow, Tracy, & Maxwell, 1995 • Whitehead, 2004

Increased Vocabulary Development

Students need to learn approximately 32,000 words between 1st and 12th grade, for an average of 7 words a day or 3,000 words per year. The typical vocabulary program teaches 700 words per year, so the remainder of words must be acquired through incidental reading (Nagy & Anderson, 1984). Wide reading is an important form of this incidental reading; it can provide students with exposure to a limitless number of new words. Furthermore, wide reading gives students multiple exposures to vocabulary terms and provides encounters with words in rich contexts, both recommendations of the NRP.

In a fascinating article titled "What Reading Does for the Mind," Cunningham and Stanovich (1998) argue that the bulk of vocabulary growth during a child's lifetime occurs through language exposure, not direct teaching. Using research by Hayes and Ahrens (1988), they analyzed the number of rare words found in a variety of sources, including printed texts, television texts, and adult speech. Cunningham and Stanovich found that exposure to the rarest words comes through books and other print materials, not through exposure to adult speech or television. They conclude that

> we should provide all children, regardless of their achievement levels, with as many reading experiences as possible...this becomes doubly imperative for precisely those children whose verbal abilities are most in need of bolstering, for it is the very act of reading that can build those capacities. (p. 8)

Greater Domain and Background Knowledge

Deep knowledge about a particular topic requires long-term immersion in an area of study, which can occur when students explore a particular topic through independent reading. By developing students' domain knowledge through early independent reading experiences, you help younger students create schemata for topics they will find in the increasingly demanding upper grade-level texts.

Students who read independently have more general knowledge and greater domain knowledge than those who do not (Cunningham & Stanovich, 1991; Guthrie & Greaney, 1991; Krashen, 2004; Stanovich & Cunningham, 1993). For example, Ravitch and Finn (1987) found that

17-year-olds who read extensively performed better on tests of history and literature than those who did not.

Success in reading depends on the ability to concentrate and sustain attention, which independent reading experiences can help develop (Block & Mangieri, 1996). This reading "stamina" is essential not only to create readers capable of attending to long passages of print such as those found on tests but also to create students who deeply engage with books, who become so engrossed in a book that they lose track of time and place.

Better Fluency and Comprehension

Independent reading experiences allow students opportunities to practice reading, so it is logical to assume that these experiences would positively affect students' abilities to read fluently with accurate pronunciation and appropriate expression. In her review of beginning reading research, Adams (1990) concludes that children's reading facility and vocabulary growth depends upon reading large amounts of text. Pikulski (2007) notes that "substantial correlational evidence shows a clear relationship between the amount students read, their reading fluency, and their reading comprehension" (p. 90). Increased reading volume has been correlated with reading comprehension performance in both low-achieving and normally achieving readers. Indeed, amount of reading is a strong predictor of reading comprehension, outweighing even intelligence, economic background, and gender (Reutzel & Hollingsworth, 1991). Conversely, low-achieving readers typically do not engage in wide reading. Their often less-than-fluent reading may result from lack of practice in reading appropriate materials (Allington, 2006).

Independent reading also contributes to comprehension development for English-language learners (ELLs). Elley and Mangubhai (1983) found that providing students with interesting books and time to read contributed significantly to students' English development and English reading comprehension when compared with classrooms that added the books but provided little emphasis on reading.

Wide reading experiences may provide a powerful accompaniment to fluency practice. In a study of second graders that compared groups of students who engaged in repeated readings and groups that engaged in repeated readings *and* wide reading, researchers found that both groups made gains in word recognition, but that only the wide reading group improved their comprehension (Kuhn, 2004). As researcher Cunningham (2005) states,

> A child who reads abundantly develops greater reading skills, a larger vocabulary and more general knowledge about the world. In return, they have increased reading comprehension, and, therefore, enjoy more pleasurable reading experiences and are encouraged to read even more. By contrast a child who rarely reads is slower in the development of reading skills and is exposed to fewer new vocabulary words and less information about the world. As a result, the child struggles more while reading and comprehends less of the text. Not surprisingly, this child derives less enjoyment from reading experiences and is less likely to choose to read in the future. (p. 63)

Improved Reading Achievement

More reading equals better reading achievement. In today's era of accountability-driven education, we can become too focused on the "bottom line"—standardized test scores. Dozens of studies confirm the relationship between the volume of independent reading that students do and reading achievement. Based on her analysis of numerous studies of recreational reading, Cullinan (2000) concludes that although correlations between the amount of reading and literacy test scores are not always statistically significant they are consistent.

According to Allington (2006), a potent relationship exists between the volume of reading and reading achievement. Students whose reading development lags behind their peers engage in far less reading. Anderson, Wilson, and Fielding's (1988) classic study of students' out-of-school reading habits demonstrates the relationship between students' reading volume and reading achievement as measured by standardized tests (see Table 4). The 155 fifth graders in the study kept logs documenting their out-of-school reading time. Students who read independently for an hour a day (4,358,000 words per year) scored at the 98th percentile on standardized reading tests. Students who reported reading an average of 4.6 minutes per day (282,000 words per year) scored at the 50th percentile. Students who did not read at all out of school scored at the 2nd percentile.

The tremendous gulf between good readers and poor readers in terms of reading volume is well demonstrated in this study. A student in the top 10 percentile reads as much in eight days as a student in the bottom

Table 4. Variation in the Amount of Independent Reading

Percentile	Independent Reading Minutes Per Day	Words Read Per Year
98	65.0	4,358,000
90	21.1	1,823,000
70	9.6	622,000
50	4.6	282,000
30	1.3	106,000
10	0.1	8,000
2	0.0	0

Note. Adapted from Anderson, R.C., Wilson, P.T., & Fielding, L.G. (1988). Growth in reading and how children spend their time outside of school. Reading Research Quarterly, 23(3), 285–303.

10 percentile reads during the entire year! Proficient fourth graders read about 500% more than less proficient ones, and struggling fourth graders needed to read three to five hours daily if they were ever to catch up (Guthrie, 2004).

The National Assessment of Educational Progress (NAEP) provides a snapshot of the reading abilities and habits of 4th, 8th, and 12th graders across the United States and is considered the gold standard of reading assessment. Results of the 2004 NAEP study (Perle, Moran, Lutkus, & Tirre, 2005) reaffirm the important role of independent reading. At every age level, students who reported reading recreationally almost every day had higher average reading scores than those who reported never or almost never reading recreationally. Even those students who reported reading once or twice a week had higher average scores than students who never or hardly ever read recreationally.

In his classic book *The Power of Reading: Insights From the Research*, Krashen (2004) describes his analysis of 41 studies of in-school free reading, sustained silent reading (SSR), and self-selected reading programs. In 38 of those studies, students who engaged in independent reading did as well or better on standardized reading tests than students who only had direct reading instruction.

Two studies of summer reading provide support for the importance of wide reading. A study by Kim (2003) looks at ethnically diverse fifth graders' summer reading and its effect on achievement. Students who read more over the summer made significantly greater gains in reading comprehension as measured by standardized tests than those students who did not. In fact, summer reading loss was largely eliminated for those students who independently read five books over the summer.

In a similar study of sixth graders from varied racial and socioeconomic groups, Heyns (1978) attempts to identify the differences between those who regressed and those who continued to learn over the summer. She found that the single activity most correlated with summer learning was reading.

Guthrie (2002) analyzes numerous studies to identify the percentage of time that should be devoted to various aspects of reading test preparation. He recommends that 40% of time be devoted to guided instruction, 20% to engaged reading, 20% to strategy instruction, 10% to motivation, and 10% to teaching test formats. He concludes that emphasis is needed on direct instruction in literacy strategies but argues that "a substantial emphasis should be placed on engaged, independent reading to learn. All reading tests require speed, fluency, and comprehension. This can only be learned in motivated, extended, engaged reading" (p. 377). It is through such reading that students gain the general knowledge they need to succeed on tests, as well as in the world.

Greater Interest in Books and Motivation to Read

Yoon's (2002) meta-analysis of independent reading studies showed that independent reading provides significant gains in reading attitude. High-interest materials are more pleasurable to students and result in their reading for longer time periods (Guthrie & Greaney, 1991). In addition, students have better comprehension of high-interest materials than they have of low-interest materials (Asher & Markell, 1974). Students are more motivated to read (Morrow & Young, 1997) and do so with greater comprehension when reading materials they find interesting (Guthrie, Schafer, Von Secker, & Alban, 2000).

Independent reading experiences that are based on the idea of student self-selection of materials can be highly motivating for students and provide rich opportunities for reading materials that have personal appeal to individual students. The opportunity to self-select materials can provide students with opportunities to engage in light reading of nonschool materials, including magazines like *Kids Discover* or *National Geographic Kids,* graphic novels, or joke and riddle books. Such materials can give students opportunities to read more books by authors they have been introduced to in the basal reader or to read a favorite teacher read-aloud on their own. According to Allington (1994), this wide reading on topics of personal interest is "the most potent factor in the development of reading processes" (p. 21). The enjoyment provided by engaging with topics of interest can open students to the pleasure of reading.

In- and Out-of-School Factors That Affect Independent Reading

Just as students' out-of-school reading contributes to their reading success, so does their in-school reading. Despite the increased emphasis on reading instruction required by No Child Left Behind, students in classrooms are not necessarily spending more time reading. Brenner, Tompkins, and Riley (2007) found that during the 90 minutes of reading/ language arts instruction in the Mississippi Reading First classrooms they studied, students spent only 18 minutes in actual reading. Other studies suggest that simply adding more reading time may support reading achievement more than additional basal reading time (Block, Cleveland, & Reed, 2005). Schools with higher achieving students usually schedule more opportunities for real reading and writing than schools with lower achieving students (Cunningham & Allington, 2007).

The use of literature in the classroom can promote student interest in books. Blatt's (1981) longitudinal study examining the classroom environments in which students learned to read found teachers were most successful in fostering reading interests when they gave students time to read, used literature to teach reading, or read aloud regularly to students. The teaching of reading occurs through the use of a basal reader in 80–90% of classrooms (Baumann, Hoffman, Duffy-Hester, & Ro, 2000), yet, support for the use of literature in the classroom comes from students themselves; research consistently indicates that students enjoy being read aloud to, enjoy reading children's literature, and prefer reading trade books to basal stories or textbooks (Ivey & Broaddus, 2001; Mendoza, 1985). Fielding, Wilson, and Anderson (1986) found that avid readers belonged to reading communities that began at home but also consisted of peers and teachers.

Hiebert, Mervar, and Person (1990) note that second graders from classrooms where use of literature was commonplace gave more detailed reasons for their book selections and had specific books in mind when they visited the library. Morrow (1983) found that kindergartners from classrooms with literature programs rated as good or excellent showed higher interest in books than students who did not. Clearly, this interest in books often translates into more time spent reading.

The Important Role of the Teacher

Independent reading time provides you with opportunities to extend and build on reading experiences created during guided reading or shared reading. It can provide teaching points for individual students or lead to additional reading in books related to titles encountered during shared or guided reading. You should guide your students' independent reading experiences in ways that helps develop the reading habit and provide differentiated independent reading guidance based on your students' reading development. The goals you have for a student who does virtually no independent reading should be different from the goals for one who is simply in a "reading rut." For the first student, consider the areas of interest as a criterion for book selection. For the high-ability reader in a rut of Encyclopedia Brown books, push the pursuit of more sophisticated mysteries like *Chasing Vermeer* (Balliett, 2004).

Block and Mangieri (2002) surveyed teachers' recreational reading practices and found that teachers with a strong knowledge of children's literature and recreational reading activities were lifelong readers themselves. These teachers provide opportunities in class for silent reading, engage students in reading a broad range of books, and give students incentives for reading at home. Sadly, 17% of the teacher respondents to their survey could not name a single activity that promoted recreational reading for students, and an additional 33% could name only one.

Applegate and Applegate (2004) found that teachers' reading habits significantly affect student achievement, motivation, and reading engagement. Teachers who do not read are less able to help students select books based on the students' interests and may not recognize the effect of their methods on student attitudes toward reading (Short & Pierce, 1990). However, those teachers who serve as explicit reading models for students and specifically associate reading with enjoyment, pleasure, and learning are more likely to inspire students to become voluntary lifelong readers (Cameron & Pierce, 1995). Finally, Morrison, Jacobs, and Swinyard (1999) learned that teachers who are enthusiastic readers are more likely to use recommended innovations in their teaching, and thus are better suited to help students become thoughtful, engaged readers.

Being closely involved with students during independent reading time is essential. The "new view" of SSR, for example, suggests that your role as a teacher has changed from passive to active (Gambrell, 2007). Asking students to read by themselves during independent reading time may not be a good use of time (Stahl, 2004). Younger students may lack the fluency required for success; older struggling readers may not engage with texts in meaningful ways. Rather than reading during SSR time, you can monitor students as they partner read, conference with students, engage them in discussions around books, and work with them to select appropriate books.

Recent experimental studies identify particular teacher instructional behaviors that contribute to making independent reading time valuable. Kuhn and colleagues (2006), for example, explored fluency development with second graders. They found that increasing the time students spend in reading appropriately challenging texts *with scaffolded instruction* led to both word reading improvement and increases in reading comprehension. Similarly, Reutzel, Jones, Fawson, and Smith (2008) found that a third grade scaffolded silent reading program was as effective as a program involving guided repeated oral readings. This scaffolding can take many different forms. It should, at a minimum, include the following: careful matching of books and readers, activities designed to motivate students to read, monitoring students during reading time, making students accountable, and providing feedback to students. These activities are described in later chapters. Block and Pressley (2007) point out that students' independent reading experiences should involve books at their recreational reading level that the teacher has introduced and that are related to classroom topics or themes. Support for this view comes from a recent experimental study that examined whether differences in independent reading time, when used in concert with a balanced reading program, could influence reading outcomes in third- and fifth-grade classrooms (Samuels & Wu, 2003). The authors found that extra reading practice time was beneficial to both high- and low-ability readers but that the books student read must match their reading ability and their ability to maintain attention.

As Block and Pressley (2007) note, "For silent reading periods to produce significant comprehension gains for all readers, teachers must perform one or more of the following actions. Teachers must monitor, intercede, reteach and assess students individually as they read silently" (p. 229). Part of this monitoring function involves ensuring that students are reading books at the proper level, scaffolding student reading experiences that ensure success, and making sure that students comprehend what they are reading.

Classroom Libraries and Reading Materials

It is difficult to overstate the importance of classroom libraries. Morrow (2003) and Neuman (1999) note that students read 50–60% more in classrooms with libraries than in classrooms without them. Studies of early readers and interviews with avid readers find that students who love to read almost always have access to books at home. Because many students today do not have that home access, it is paramount that all students be provided with books in the classroom (Fractor, Woodruff, Martinez, & Teale, 1993). Students with ready access to books in their schools and classrooms are far more likely to read than students who don't have this access (Kim, 2003).

Snow and her colleagues (Snow, Barnes, Chandler, Goodman, & Hemphill, 1991) describe factors that affected the literacy achievement of elementary school students (second, fourth, and sixth graders) from low-income families. They found that students who were in classrooms that provided access to challenging and stimulating literacy materials, including trade books that represented a wide range of difficulty levels, showed more substantial gains in vocabulary and word recognition than students who were not. This study and others conclude that rich literacy environments and a teacher's "exploitation of instructional strategies and materials that go beyond the basics of teaching reading can compensate for less than ideal home environments" (Reutzel & Hollingsworth, 1991, p. 86).

The number of books in the classroom also seems to matter. In a study of 32 schools in Maryland, for example, Guthrie and colleagues (2000) found that an abundance of trade books in the classroom predicted gains on statewide reading, writing, and science tests. According to Krashen (2004), having more books in the classroom leads to more voluntary reading, which in turn results in higher achievement. As Ramos and Krashen (1998) state,

> Providing interesting books for children is a powerful incentive for reading, perhaps the most powerful incentive possible. This conclusion is consistent with research showing that extrinsic incentives for reading have not been successful, while improving access to books has been successful in encouraging reading. (p. 614)

School Libraries

Lance, Welborn, and Hamilton-Pennell (1993) found a positive correlation among school library expenditures, the role of the librarian, and student achievement. Furthermore, Sinclair-Tarr and Tarr (2007) examined data from 4,022 California schools at the elementary, middle, and high school levels. They found statistically significant relationships between the presence of a school library and student achievement on both the English language arts and mathematics California Standards Tests at the elementary and middle levels. At the elementary level, particular library features including collection size, hours of operation, video collection, and library skills programs were correlated with student achievement.

Krashen (2004) concludes from a variety of studies that students obtain a large percentage of reading material from the school library. Greater access to books and libraries with professional librarians correlates with higher reading achievement scores. Libraries with larger, high-quality collections, comfortable reading environments, and certified librarians produce students with better reading achievement. Two studies (Krashen, 1995; McQuillan, 1998) that examined the relationship between school libraries and student scores on the NAEP found that the number of books per student in the school library was a strong predictor of student test scores on the NAEP. These studies confirm the importance of access to books and demonstrate that classroom libraries, while important, are not enough.

The Home and Community

Early readers come from homes where parents read to them, give help with reading and writing, often read themselves, and make use of the public library. Books and writing materials are present in these homes, and reading is a valued activity (Durkin, 1966). Morrow (1983) notes that "before the child gets to school many background characteristics that have been linked to high and low interest in literature have been established" (p. 229). Furthermore, children's literacy development depends to a large extent on what adult caregivers, whether parents or preschool teachers, do to engage students. Studies in daycare centers, for example, reveal that students in preschools where teachers regularly read to student, provide access to books, and involve students in reading and writing activities engage in more literacy behaviors than students who do not have these experiences (Morrow, 1993).

Unfortunately, many students are not provided with early literacy experiences at home. This makes it incumbent upon teachers at every level to involve families in ways that help them understand the importance of reading at home. Making families part of school literacy programs can help to ensure that students become successful readers and writers (Tabors, Snow, & Dickinson, 2001; Wasik, 2004). Helping parents to understand the value of in-home reading is key, too. Parents know their children better than anyone else, and this knowledge can give them real power in terms of helping their children select books of compelling personal interest. In Appendix B, you will find three reproducible handouts for parents: (1) tips for setting up a home library, (2) guidelines for helping children select appropriate reading materials, and (3) suggestions for promoting interest in content area reading.

Communities too can help to support independent readers with incentive programs that provide prizes and other rewards to students who succeed in reading a specified number of books. These programs often involve partnerships with community organizations, including public libraries, local businesses, service organizations, and so on. Many communities sponsor book drives that provide students in low-income schools with books for independent reading.

Public libraries and librarians are critical partners in promoting independent reading (Cullinan, 2000). Libraries provide myriad programs for promoting independent reading, often in concert with school districts. Libraries often promote family literacy, offer tutoring services, partner with Head Start, or provide special programs and services to promote reading among adolescents. Summer reading programs, which help ensure that students continue to read outside of school, are found in many public libraries.

Framework for an Independent Reading Program

This book is based on the idea that independent reading is not just something that happens in a single classroom or at home. A comprehensive program designed to promote independent reading is multifaceted; even though such a program depends upon individual teachers and students, it also depends upon the principal, the school librarian, parents, and the community if it is to be successful. Fountas and Pinnell (2001) provide guidelines for thinking about structured independent reading, suggesting these five key elements:

1. Teachers guide student text selections.
2. Students record what they read.
3. Students reflect on their reading.
4. Teachers and students engage in minilessons and discussions.
5. Teachers do not read during the block.

The framework for an independent reading program described in this book builds on and extends the Fountas and Pinnell (2001) principles for classroom-based independent reading experiences. We believe that an independent reading program should become an integral part of a balanced reading program, and to be successful such a program must include the following:

- Supportive reading environments
- Access to interesting books and reading materials
- Structured time for engaging with texts
- Accountability
- Active engagement by teachers
- Family and community connections

An independent reading program cannot succeed unless it provides young readers with *supportive reading environments*. Environment is crucial not only at the classroom level but also across the entire school. Access to books, book displays, comfortable chairs, and other accoutrements can make the difference in whether students engage with books. Providing book advertisements and displays in display cases around the school is one way to create a book-friendly environment. The school library assumes a critical role in this area.

Schoolwide reading programs help to create a supportive environment for reading. Whether taking the form of SSR, incentive programs, or young authors programs, involvement in reading that extends beyond individual classrooms and teachers is essential.

An effective schoolwide independent reading program provides students with *access to interesting books and reading materials.* Students should have daily access to books and other print materials found in a well-stocked classroom library—one that contains at least 100 titles representing a variety of genres. Students should have contact with books located not only on the shelves of the classroom library but also in book displays, spinning racks, and in myriad locations around the classroom. School libraries extend this access to a broader range of materials, providing far more choices than are possible in a classroom library.

Access to books is not enough, however. Students need access to books with appeal. Confining students' choices to award-winning titles, no matter how excellent, still limits choices and denies students the opportunity to select books that matter to them. A range of texts, including light reading materials such as magazines, graphic novels, and joke and riddle books, is essential if texts are to captivate reluctant readers and reluctant independent readers. (See Chapter 2 for more suggestions on creating an engaging reading environment.)

A third component of a successful independent reading program is *structured time for engaging with texts.* This includes time for you to read aloud, provide brief minilessons related to independent reading, confer with students, and assess students' progress as independent readers. Both time for reading and time for talking about texts are essential components of effective independent reading, and we discuss each briefly.

To make sure students receive enough time for reading, at least 60 minutes per day in school and 20 minutes per day out of school should be provided. In-school reading can occur any time that is convenient for teachers and students: while guided reading groups are meeting, during a specified SSR or learning center time, or during library visits, to name a few. These experiences need to occur during reading time, as well as during content area reading classes (see Chapter 5). Out-of-school reading time is a specific part of assigned homework, ideally accomplished with the help and support of the parents or caregivers. (Chapter 3 provides more information on how to structure an independent reading program.)

Time for talking about texts should be made at least twice a week for 20 minutes. This talk about text is designed to create a classroom community centered on reading and books with a variety of engagement activities such as teacher–student book talks, paired sharing of books, sharing videos and websites about books and authors, or discussions on read-alouds. Responses to independent reading can go beyond talking: Artistic, musical, or dramatic responses to text can creatively extend reading experiences and provide rich opportunities for students to share their books with one another, thus creating motivation for reading for all. (Chapter 4 provides many ideas for helping students respond to their independent reading.)

Accountability is key to a successful reading program, even though student self-assessment and teacher assessment also take time. Students must be held accountable for their independent reading on a daily basis by maintaining daily reading logs, sharing with their teachers and peers, completing journal entries, or responding to reading through writing, speaking, and listening. You should maintain records about student behaviors during independent reading time by completing rubrics, checklists, and other formal and informal assessments. Regularly complete attitude and interest surveys with students to determine their interests so that meaningful decisions about book choices can be made.

Active engagement by teachers is another critical component of a successful independent reading program. As mentioned previously, you should be an active participant during independent reading time, guiding students as they select books, providing minilessons designed to heighten student understanding, orchestrating student responses to the texts that they choose, and coordinating student record-keeping. Sometimes you might read silently to model what good readers do during independent reading time, but you should be encouraging the love of reading on a daily basis.

Effective independent reading programs create meaningful *family and community connections*. Parents and communities should be active partners in the independent reading program and participate regularly in the reading lives of students. Successful programs provide frequent and structured opportunities for parental and community involvement, which we discuss briefly.

Parental involvement can be established by inviting parents and caregivers to engage with their children in frequent, structured activities related to independent reading. At-home independent reading programs can benefit students (Padak & Rasinski, 2003). However, it is necessary for schools to teach parents how to help their children become lifelong readers. Teaching parents how to read aloud, how to do paired reading with children, or how to listen to children's read-alouds provides concrete ways for parents to support and extend students' reading development.

Community involvement, such as engaging the public library, local government, museums, area businesses, and other groups in supporting students' reading, can pay big dividends for schools. Such efforts strengthen school–community ties and unite these groups in working toward a common goal. Programs like the San Diego School in the Park, for example, engage students in extended study at the San Diego Zoo, the Natural History Museum, and the Timken Museum of Art. These experiences provide starting points for stimulating student interest and can lead to rich independent reading experiences that can extend and deepen student learning.

Independent reading programs can help to ensure that students and families make time for reading. Such programs can make a difference in students' lives and contribute to their academic growth, their enthusiasm for books, and their lifelong learning. No doubt you feel enormous pressure to teach students the reading skills essential to a balanced literacy program. All too often, reading progress is only measured by test scores. However, the goal of reading instruction must extend further. As Morrow (2003) points out, "The benefits of voluntary reading as intellectual stimulation and growth, acculturation, and general transfer of information are a matter of long-range development rather than of an immediate payoff" (p. 864). For this reason, the development of independent readers cannot be viewed as an optional activity but rather as an integral part to every classroom. It is essential to the development of an informed citizenry, engaged learners, and students who are prepared to meet the literacy demands of the 21st century.

Richard L. Allington is a professor of education at the University of Tennessee. He was an elementary school classroom teacher and a Title I director in poor, rural schools prior to beginning his career as a teacher educator and instructional researcher. His research interests include reading/learning disabilities and effective instruction, especially in classroom settings. His publications include more than 100 articles, chapters, monographs, and books. Allington has served as president of the National Reading Conference and the International Reading Association.

Terrell Young: In your book, *What Really Matters in Response to Intervention: Research-Based Designs* (Allington, 2009b), you make a compelling case about the importance of matching reader and text level. You suggest that in order for students to have "high success reading" they should read materials with 99–100% accuracy for independent reading. Is this equally important to all students or more so for struggling readers?

Richard Allington: It's for everybody. Ninety-nine percent accuracy sounds high until you actually start thinking about it. Most people wouldn't read a book they could only read with 99% accuracy. In an adult novel, say a John Grisham novel, that's the equivalent of 3 or 4 words on every page you couldn't pronounce and didn't know what they meant. Or in a 20- or 30-page first chapter you'd have, perhaps 100, 120 words you couldn't read, and in the real world nobody—no skilled reader—actually attempts that kind of reading except if they're looking for a cure for spinal cancer and the only thing they can find to read are medical journals. But most of us would just give up on those if they contained lots of words we didn't recognize and go searching on the Web for something that was easier.

So the 99% accuracy is the standard, but probably by fourth grade it should be a 99.9% standard. And by the time we reach high school and college level, it's probably a 99.999% standard of accuracy.

TY: That supports what Emmet Betts said a long time ago about lots of easy reading makes reading easy.

RA: Betts is one of my main standbys because his work back in the 1940s first established the 99% accuracy for what he called independent reading, but that's been sort of mistakenly translated into independent reading or recreational reading as opposed to *all* of the reading you do outside of a small guided reading group. And even there his original work suggested that 97% or 98% accuracy was the optimum for instructional level. He ultimately lowered that to 95% in part because what he found was that when teachers were doing guided reading, often in the before-reading activities, they introduced key vocabulary as well as building some background knowledge, which meant that once the kids were given the text, they could actually read it at the 99% accuracy level. And it was probably a mistake for him to do that because now suddenly we have generations of teachers who've learned that 95% percent accuracy is fine, and they tend to see it as fine if it's instructional level, but that's also seen as the reading kids are required to do independently as opposed to a small guided reading group. And I just don't know many content area teachers in upper grade levels who actually have small guided reading groups.

TY: Many teachers request that parents monitor their children's independent reading at home but feel that the reading does not really take place even when many of the parents sign forms indicating that it has. What is your best advice for teachers for getting kids to read at home and for gaining parents' support for such reading?

RA: My first advice is don't expect parents to help you, period. It's just too easy to say, "The parents weren't supportive and that's the reason the kid didn't read." The reason children don't read during the summer or independently outside of school anywhere is that nobody's ever helped them find a book that they were interested in; a book they could actually read. We have lots of required readings or assigned readings but try to find a 4th-grade teacher or 8th-grade or a 10th-grade English teacher who allows children to pick books they're interested in, much less books that they can actually read—it just doesn't happen. We have all these strategies for helping kids cope with texts they can't read, but we don't have the fundamental strategy, which is don't put a book in their hands that's hard or a book that's boring. If you don't know any books that students in your classroom would want to read, then you probably shouldn't be teaching, because it means you haven't read very widely in your field. But we don't have that as a requirement for teachers, that they actually have read widely and particularly read widely in their fields.

The domination of the one-size-fits-all curriculum framework, particularly as exemplified in textbook adoption states, is the major reason why so many kids don't do well in school.

TY: I was surprised at the number of books I read in high school that my children read as well.

RA: Yes, me, too—only in high school I didn't read them. But given the array of titles—and we've seen an explosion of children's publishing and adolescent publishing in the last 20 years—given the array of titles that are available in every subject area, virtually, the fact that most classrooms don't have a classroom library where they have 1,000 titles at different levels of difficulty that cover a variety of topics says more about the failings of teachers and our school systems than it does about the quality of the kids who are showing up.

I challenge teachers when I speak by saying, "You, give me your two most disaffected readers, the two kids that hate reading the most, and give me $100 and let me take them to the local bookstore. I'll have them sitting on the floor reading—I'll have them reading in the backseat of the car on the way home." It's not that hard to find things that kids will actually read, it's just hard to find those things in schools.

We recently concluded a study (Allington et al., 2007) on summer reading loss. The question was, if we gave kids the option of choosing from about 500 book titles—book titles that represented the range of reading difficulties that were in this 17-school sample that had first grade, second grade, third grade, or fourth grade—if kids picked the novels and we gave them to them on the last day of school, would the kids read them? And if they read the books, would it have any effect on their reading achievement? And the answer in both cases was yes. The vast majority of kids read the novels they picked, and the effect size across the whole sample was equal to the effect size that Harris Cooper (Cooper, Charlton, Valentine, & Muhlenbruck, 2000) calculated for attending summer school from his meta-analysis of some 39 studies of summer school effects.

So the basic point is that if you give kids books they actually can read and want to read, you can avoid sending kids to summer school, and you can provide those books. We gave each kid a dozen books each summer at a total cost of about $45 a kid per year, or about $130 for the three-year period, which pales in comparison to the $3,000 per kid that a good summer school will cost. And the better news, perhaps, is that we had book logs that the kids filled in; we'd asked them to draw a picture of their favorite scene after they finished the book and write a sentence or two about the book, and then just answer two questions: (1) was it easy, about right, or too hard, and (2) was it boring, OK, or really interesting? Across the sample only about 20% of the kids actually completed their book logs and mailed them in, but in that 20% of the kids, the effect size was twice as large as going to summer school. So at least for the kids who we know actually read their books, the overall impact sort of verifies what Keith Stanovich (e.g., Cunningham & Stanovich, 1998; Stanovich, 1986), David Share (e.g., de Jong & Share, 2007; Share, 1999), and Anne Cunningham (2006) have been writing about for decades on the influence of independent, wide reading on reading achievement.

It's similar to what Melanie Kuhn (2004) has recently reported in terms of comparing repeated readings with what she calls the "just reading" phenomenon, where poor readers are put in two groups, and one group does repeated readings for 30 minutes a day trying to read to a criterion, and another group just reads a self-selected book for 30 minutes a day. And the overall finding was that the self-selected reading actually at least equaled repeated readings in the development of fluency. Self-selected reading was better than repeated readings on word recognition and vocabulary and comprehension. And so, we've got lots of folks around the country thinking that repeated readings is a strategy that they need to be using, when in fact it looks like just allowing kids the opportunity to read books they *want* to read and they *can* read works even better than repeated readings at fostering reading growth.

Since the National Reading Panel interpretations came out that suggested it was a waste of time to let kids read independently during school and maybe reading outside of school would be a better idea, lots of schools have been more likely to adopt repeated readings and phonics study than to actually encourage kids to spend part of the school day reading. The problem with the argument for out-of-school reading wouldn't be so bad if they'd also said, "But in order to do this, you're going to have to make sure that you have hundreds of book titles, and if somebody can't find a book title they want to read, you need to take them to [a bookstore or library] or someplace and find a book for them." But the fact that poor kids don't own books and by and large don't even have books and magazine in their homes, while middle class kids on average have 100 age-appropriate books in their home never seems to strike anyone as the real problem, as opposed to not enough phonics being the real problem.

But one of the questions that you had asked about—what were three or four things that teachers could do to increase the amount of reading their kids do during the summer or just during out of school periods, evenings, or weekends? And I think the number one and the single most important factor is that they make sure kids have easy access to a wide range of texts they can read, and texts that they're interested in reading. And I'd like to say, "Go to your school library," but school libraries aren't typically a place to find a book that kids want to read.

And besides that, librarians tend to put books up on the shelf stacked with their spines out as a way of protecting the books from children. And so if you were a child wanting something to read, you wouldn't find it in most libraries unless you knew what you wanted to read and you could tell the librarian and then she could use her secret ways to find you a book on that topic. If you contrast what an average library looks like to what the average children's bookstore looks like, you find out pretty quickly that bookstores are much more likely to have books displayed face out—front cover out—than libraries are. And the places that probably sell the most books per person, in my view, are the little shops in the airports where you can buy yourself a Coke as well as a paperback novel, and they always have the books cover out, and the reason they do is they want people to buy them. If you want kids to read books, then you need to show them covers and you can't have the standard school library cover, which is devoid of any illustration or any of the short summaries and so on that you find in the back of paperback books. So that's my general rule of thumb: in a fourth-grade classroom you probably need 500 to 1,000 titles to find books for 90% of the kids. The other 10% of the kids you're going to have to go outside your classroom, and you may have to go to the bookstore, not the library, to help find them.

Furthermore, I think that we have completely overlooked is what Arthur Applebee (Applebee, Langer, Nystrand, & Gamoran, 2003) and Marty Nystrand (2006) have called literate conversation, and that's simply talking about the book that you're reading. We have good evidence from their work that adding 5 or 10 minutes an hour of conversation time in which kids talk to each other or talk to the teacher about the books that they're reading both improves their understanding of the books that they're reading and improves their reading comprehension test scores better than anything anybody else has created. Yet the number of classrooms where kids are talking to each other about what they're reading, or even classrooms where they're talking to their teacher in a conversational manner is slim to none. Nystrand's work found that at best perhaps 10% of the high school English teachers in his large-scale study ever engaged in literate conversations with their students. Instead, what teachers do is interrogate students—they ask questions they know the answers to. And often teachers ask the most trivial questions and never is conversation in the way that you and I might talk about, you know, an op-ed piece that we'd read today in the paper, or talk about a novel that you were reading and I'd already read, and so on. Those types of conversations just don't take place in classroom, but they should. And if teachers want kids to read widely, giving them the opportunity to talk to other kids and to the teacher about it is another strategy that needs to be put in place.

TY: I find that also has a high recreational reading potential, too, because as kids hear one person share a book, then they also want to read that book as well.

RA: Yes, if you think about how many books in the past year that you've read that you just found by yourself, it's pretty slim, particularly from recreational or independent reading books only. People recommend books to you. People tell you about a book they're reading. And when I say "people," I mean sometimes it's somebody on television talking about a book. It's not necessarily the teacher teaching next door to you, but it's when somebody says, "This is the best book I've ever read," that you suddenly start to think, "Well, hmm, maybe I should read that, too." And the next thing you know you're reading the book. It's that sort of word of mouth that makes books bestsellers—that and an Oprah endorsement. But Oprah usually talks about the books, and people at home think that she's talking to them.

Another general rule I would put in place is don't give kids assignments to write about the book or to answer a series of questions about the book, and so on. Again, let's go back to the real world. Once you graduate from school, how many times does someone give you a quiz on the book that you're reading? And even in the medical industry doctors read medical journals, but no one quizzes them on what they read. No one, in fact, even says, "I don't think you actually read it, so therefore you get a D and a cut in your salary."

And also, I'd say, another thing that's popular in schools that should be ended is providing a list of books that kids must read. I mean, if you want to make sure no one will read those books have the school endorse them. If you wanted a plan for increasing the reading of books, you could have individual kids talk about books that they've read that they really liked and why they liked them, and put the video clips on your website. And tell parents, "If you're looking for books for 9-year-olds, go to this spot on the website and listen to some titles that different kids like—and sit with your child and see if one of those books sounds like a book they'd like to read. But if you don't find one there, take them to the library or the bookstore and see if you can find a book they really like to read." Because it doesn't matter if teachers give you assignments or not—as I learned a long time ago, you can always find someone else to do your assignments. If the teachers say, "Everybody has to read *Sarah, Plain and Tall* (MacLachlan, 1985)" then boys are going to be shortchanged compared with girls because it's a girl-oriented book, which is a basic problem with most of the books that schools recommend, because books that boys like to read are seen as inappropriate in topic and content and style and form. So it's no wonder that the majority of our struggling readers are boys.

TY: As students get older, the size of the books they read varies greatly. How much would you recommend that kids read over the summer to prevent summer reading loss at first, third, and fifth grade?

RA: We know from the work that we've done in first grade that kids probably need to read 15 to 25 books every summer, and I say that in part because if you read at 100 words a minute, which is a good reading rate for, say, a second grader, it'll take you about 10 minutes to read a Frog and Toad book. Now there really aren't very many books at the fourth-grade level that you can read in 10 minutes.

By third-grade level, when you get up to books like—oh, I don't know—

TY: *Stone Fox* (Gardiner, 1980)?

RA: Like *Stone Fox*—good example—the book is longer, more words, more pages, and it takes a kid reading at 100 or 200 words a minute or, let's say, 150 words a minute, you know, maybe two or three hours to read *Stone Fox*. And by the time you get to fifth grade, where you've got *Island of the Blue Dolphins* (O'Dell, 1960), which is even longer and we've got work from what Kim (2004, 2006) has done with upper elementary grade kids that says basically if they read five books during the summer you can predict that their reading skills will have grown. If they read zero books or one book during the summer, you can predict that their reading skills declined over the summer. And in the middle, between that—two to four books—you can't really predict. Some of those kids stay even, some fall back, and some gain a little bit. But five or six books was the target for his fifth- and sixth-grade study because when kids read that many books they actually experienced positive growth in reading achievement.

TY: So for third graders would you say something like between 6 and 10?

RA: I'd say something between 10 and 15. By fifth grade it's probably 5 to 10.

TY: What do you view as the role of instruction during independent reading time?

RA: I would just argue the only instruction that I think you need is literate conversation while the child's reading or after he's finished reading. And it's not conversation to teach the child something, it's the conversation where the child can teach you something.

Different kids like different books, and different kids reading the same book don't all get the same understanding from it. And there are times in which the literate conversation will give you an insight into a book that you'd never had before, probably because you aren't 10. But it can also give you insights into books that—where kids just don't simply have the background knowledge to understand them. But it's during the literate conversation periods where kids are asked to summarize and paraphrase what they've read, and you can't find two better activities for kids—for fostering kids' comprehension than summarization and paraphrasing—not that either of those are done much in school. But it's a good start for helping kids understand how literate people actually read and think about their reading.

TY: Is there something you would like to address that I failed to ask?

RA: Yes, there is. The question for teachers, principals, and for superintendents, and perhaps for research teams, is how many books does your current curriculum and the classroom library and the school library actually have that the struggling readers in your class will be able to read and will want to read? And if the—the point is my 4th-grade or 8th-grade or 10th-grade social studies class has a single grade-level textbook, then it's no wonder that your struggling readers are struggling. I mean, we can't solve struggling readers' problems by providing them 30 minutes a day of work in a group of seven or nine kids, working with a paraprofessional on a phonics worksheet. Now why that hasn't occurred to most school districts is beyond me, but when you see kids sitting for six hours a day in classrooms with their desks filled with books they can't read, the answer to why they aren't learning to read becomes pretty obvious. They don't have any opportunity to actually learn to read. If you don't have a classroom library, say you're teaching 6th grade and you've got kids still reading at the 3rd-grade level or below, if you don't have a classroom library where at least a third of your books are written at the 3rd-grade level or below, then we know what the problem is. If you have a 6th-grade language arts curriculum that doesn't have books written below the 3rd-grade level, we know what the problem is. If your school library at your middle school doesn't have a bunch of books below the 3rd-grade level, then we know what the problem is—and the problem isn't the struggling readers. The problem in this case is the school. The school isn't designed to actually teach those kids anything. The school is designed to teach the high-achieving kids, and that's the way most schools are.

CHAPTER 2

How to Create a Classroom Library That Makes a Difference

Classroom libraries play a preeminent role in creating and supporting young readers. Even in schools with excellent library media centers, your classroom library provides a focal point for literacy learning. First and foremost, classroom libraries provide ready access to books, which can promote independent reading. Students are likely to spend more time reading when they are in classrooms with adequate classroom libraries (Allington & Cunningham, 2007; Krashen, 1998).

Second, quality classroom libraries confirm the central role that books and literacy play in the classroom. They are a visible representation of your commitment to creating students who read beyond the textbook and continue long after the bell has rung. In addition, quality classroom libraries demonstrate your conviction that the goal of creating lifelong readers is important. Routman (2003) attests to the significance of classroom libraries: "Classroom libraries are a literacy necessity; they are integral to successful teaching and learning and must become a top priority if our students are to become thriving, engaged readers" (p. 64).

Because many students today do not have access to books, it is paramount that all students be provided with books in the classroom (Fractor et al., 1993). According to Neuman (1999), children in high-income areas have 4,000 times the number of books available to them than children in low-income areas. Many factors contribute to this: Children in high-income areas have more books in their homes, more access to books in public libraries, and more opportunity to find books in the community— even in places such as grocery stores. Classroom libraries, however, can help to level the playing field for children of poverty, providing them with the access to books that they need and deserve.

Students need access to a range of reading materials, and trade books provide a veritable mother lode of fiction and nonfiction works that connect to most curricular areas. Trade books, as distinguished from textbooks, are published for distribution to the general public through booksellers. Trade books are informative, entertaining, and have built-in appeal for people of all ages. Whether picture book, fiction, nonfiction, or poetry, trade books have the potential to provide students with intense involvement in a subject, and the power to develop in-depth understanding of virtually every topic in the curriculum.

Students who have ready access to books in their classrooms have better attitudes about reading, reading achievement, and comprehension. Moreover, students are likely to spend more time reading when they are in classrooms with adequate classroom libraries (Allington & McGill-Franzen, 2003; Krashen, 1998; Neuman & Celano, 2001; Routman, 2003; Young & Moss, 2006). Indeed, both Morrow (2003) and Neuman (1999) found that students read 50–60% more in classrooms with libraries than in those without them. As discussed in Chapter 1, this increase in reading volume can contribute to gains in reading achievement.

Classroom libraries perform a host of functions and purposes. Mooney (2004) notes,

> Throughout any classroom day, students need access to material that provokes thought, offers comfort, confirms who they are and excites them about what they might become, values their culture, broadens their understandings and extends their knowledge, and enables them to pursue interests and complete assignments. (p. 78)

Mooney's words should serve as your classroom library mission statement.

Creating the Space: Building a Library From the Ground Up

Time and effort are required to set up the area, select the books, and prepare students to use the library. Another critical ingredient is patience: Outstanding classroom libraries do not just happen. Your library will grow in time as you and your students help to nurture and maintain it.

Not only are the books—what they offer and the quality of their content—important, but so are the ways in which you organize and make accessible the books to your students. Poorly organized libraries make it difficult for students to meet their literacy needs. Likewise, a library that is shabby in appearance presents reading as a less-than-attractive option

(Mooney, 2004). Cunningham and Allington (2006), Routman (2003), and Tunnell and Jacobs (2008) suggest that effective library areas have certain characteristics that encourage voluntary reading:

- Attractive and accessible areas
- Areas large enough to hold four or five students at a time
- Cozy seating
- A wide variety of texts, including picture books, nonfiction, poetry, and children's magazines
- Some books available in students' home languages
- Featured books displayed on open-faced shelves
- Selections rotated throughout the school year
- A listening center where students can read along with selected books
- Simple procedures for checking books out

Table 5 offers a checklist for evaluating your classroom library and the next sections provide more detailed suggestions.

Physical Space

The success of your classroom library depends largely on creating an attractive space. To create an area that provides a focal point for literacy learning, you need to define a specific space for the library and involve students in naming it. Classroom dividers, rugs, or furniture arrangements can help to mark the library space, which should be large enough for four or five students to use at a time.

Comfortable furniture helps to create a welcoming classroom library. Beanbag chairs, pillows, couches, and other furnishings can create a cozy setting that encourages engagement with books. Plants, flowers, posters, and other decorative accessories also contribute to the atmosphere. You can involve your students in the decorating process by having them create art for the area. Or you can provide unique places for reading, such as bathtubs or even a canoe. Many publishers provide free posters promoting their books, which you can use to decorate the walls of the library and spark student interest in these titles. The American Library Association's (ALA) online store sells the well-known READ posters featuring celebrities who promote reading (www.alastore.ala.org).

Table 5. Classroom Library Checklist

Characteristic	Yes	Making Progress	No
Range of nonfiction text with lots of expository text			
Range of fiction, including realistic fiction, historical fiction, fantasy, etc.			
Assortment of poetry			
50/50 balance of nonfiction/fiction			
Balance of "boy" and "girl" books			
Varied cultural representation in books			
Range of reading levels			
At least seven books per child			
New books added regularly			
Multiple copies of selected titles			
Face-out presentation of many books			
Simple method for materials check in and out			
Comfortable seating or carpeting			
Partitioned on two sides			
Space is organized effectively			
Space is large enough for four or five students			
Contains puppets, flannel board, other props, and writing utensils			
Contains an assortment of magazines			
Contains books on CD, tape, or computer with headsets			
Internet access			
Book displays			
Centers			

Note. Adapted from Kletzien, S.B., & Dreher, M.J. (2004). *Informational text in K–3 classrooms: Helping children read and write.* Newark, DE: International Reading Association.

Bookshelves make it possible to organize, store, and display books effectively in the classroom library. Open shelves can be created easily with bricks and boards or purchased inexpensively. Milk crates also make great bookshelves. In addition to or instead of bookshelves, you can use bins or baskets for book storage and display. In this way, students can gain experience in sorting and categorizing books by genre.

Book Displays. Just as department stores use attractive displays to sell merchandise, you can use displays to sell students on books and reading; packing crates, easels, chairs, and cardboard boxes are all good ways to showcase books. Students need to see more than just the spine of the book, so display books with the covers visible or with particular illustrations bookmarked, which can heighten interest in particular titles. Small picture easels are perfect for displaying books in this way, and bent coat hangers can hold pages open to an interesting photograph or section. Displaying books in strategic locations around the room can also prompt students to read. Placing a book about fish near the class aquarium or one about gerbils near the gerbil cage can prompt students to learn more about classroom pets, for example. Displays might feature book award winners, series books, nonfiction or poetry titles, students' favorite books, a book of the week, unit connections, or book/movie tie-ins like *The Tale of Despereaux: Being the Story of a Mouse, a Princess, Some Soup, and a Spool of Thread* (DiCamillo, 2004) or *Fantastic Mr. Fox* (Dahl, 2002).

You can create a book display that centers on awards given to children's favorite books, provides a brief history of the award, and showcases particular winning titles, such *Al Capone Does My Shirts* (Choldenko, 2004) for older students and *My Lucky Day* (Kasza, 2005) for younger ones. Students could create written reviews of these books, which you can add to the display later. Some displays can last until students take the books home to read; others may contain books suitable for classroom reading only.

Library Centers. You can further organize your classroom library into specific centers that capitalize on the books present in the library and further engage students in literacy learning activities. Here are a few examples:

- A storytelling center might contain folk tales and fairy tales such as *The Ugly Duckling* (Mitchell, 2007) along with flannel boards and felt characters or puppets that students can use to retell the story.
- A listening center can include audio recordings of children's books and headphones for listening. Students might listen to books read aloud online at websites like Storyline Online (www.storylineonline.net).

- A writing center could feature books such as *Love That Dog* (Creech, 2001) or *Sahara Special* (Codell, 2003), which focus on characters who write—whether in diaries, poems, or letters. Add stationery, envelopes, markers, and a range of writing materials to this center so students can draft letters to the characters, create book reviews, or write about books to their friends in buddy journals.

- An art center could feature the books of students' favorite artists, such as Eric Carle or Lois Ehlert for younger students and Brian Selznick or David Wiesner for older ones. This center could be stocked with paints, stamps, paper, and other materials students could use to explore the artistic styles of particular artists. Students might enjoy perusing the spectacular pop-up books of Robert Sabuda and checking out his website at www.robertsabuda.com, which explains how to create pop-up books. These books could then become part of the classroom collection.

- An author center might focus on two or three notable authors at a time. Nonfiction authors, for example, might include Russell Freedman, Sandra Markle, or Kathleen Krull. This center might also focus on local authors or lesser known authors who students might not learn about without your direction. Publishers' brochures and catalogs about authors and their work, author contact information, website materials, DVDs about the author, and copies of authors' books could become part of this center. Furthermore, students could view videocasts or podcasts about favorite authors such as those available from the Meet the Author section of the Reading Rockets website (www.readingrockets.org/podcasts/authors).

- A how-to and activity center could engage students in completing tasks described in craft books, science experiment books, and more. Stock this center with books and the materials necessary for completing the activities explained in them. Books about drawing from Ed Emberley might entice artistically inclined students. The NatureCraft series of books—*Look What I Did With a Leaf!* (Sohi, 1995) and *Look What I Did With a Shell!* (Sohi, 2002)—might engage students who enjoy crafts because they teach students ways to create pictures of animals with different types of leaves and shells.

Managing and Organizing the Collection

Readers appreciate materials that are organized in a user-friendly way. How can we best arrange materials so that students can easily locate them? Reutzel and Fawson (2002) and Reutzel and Gali (1998) make the following suggestions:

- Post a map by the classroom library that describes its layout.
- Display resources with covers facing out on bookshelf tops, windowsills, vinyl rain gutters, and rotating wire racks.
- Place information on shelves related to topics, themes, genres, reading levels, and best books.
- Use posters and whiteboards (created by you or your students) to facilitate students' selection of materials.
- Use graphic organizers that demonstrate connections among materials to increase students' awareness of similar materials and give students opportunities to include their own selections.
- Organize resources around interests, series, authors, or characters.
- Place books at students' eye level or below.

When you make classroom libraries more appealing and accessible, you increase the chances that students feel comfortable during their library visits.

Jones (2006) describes the student-involved library, in which students themselves determine the organization of classroom library books. She outlines a series of 7 steps that can engage students of all ages in categorizing library books over time:

1. Talk to the students about categorizing books and model how to do this.
2. Have your students identify the way they want to categorize the books.
3. Place the students into small groups, and give each group a stack of books. Have them place these books into the chosen categories.
4. Have students discuss how they would categorize their selection of books with the members of their group. Facilitate the discussion by providing feedback.

5. After 10–15 minutes, have each group reveal how they categorize the books they were given. Let students discuss whether the books make sense in the categories in which they were placed. Once the class is in agreement, place the books into bins and label the bins by name or by using a picture label.

6. Place the bins around the room so that students can easily access them.

7. Create a book key with your students that lists each category and its color code. In this way, there is a guide for the different categories in the library.

Managing a classroom library requires that you work with your students to create rules and procedures that ensure a user-friendly system. It might help to appoint a weekly student librarian who is responsible for checking books in and out. Students themselves can create check-out cards and organize a system that involves date-stamping and storing the cards until the book is returned. Or you might prefer a more informal system such as maintaining a notebook that students can use to record their names, the date, and the title of the books they check out. When students return a book, they cross off their names.

Helping Students Find Just Right Books

Matching students with just right books is a perennial difficulty. Students should engage with books that provide just the right balance between challenge and support. Studies indicate that below-average readers most often choose books that are well beyond their reading levels while more capable readers most often select titles that correspond with their reading abilities (Reutzel & Fawson, 2002).

The process of determining which book is right for a student's independent reading can be daunting. Experts and publishers have developed a variety of systems for leveling books according to difficulty. These systems base the difficulty of a particular book on a range of factors, including the number of words in the book, the number of words on a page, print features, content, vocabulary, and text structures. A letter of the alphabet is assigned to a book based on its difficulty. Unfortunately, these systems are not consistent across publishers, which often creates confusion.

Readability formulas provide another means of gauging the difficulty of a book. These formulas determine the difficulty of a book based on the length of sentences in the text and the number of syllables per sentence. The formula yields an approximate grade level for the book. For example, the back cover of a children's book may say *RL 5.3*, which indicates that the book is written at approximately a fifth-grade, third-month level. This, however, does not mean that this book would be appropriate for every fifth grader, because the typical span of reading abilities in a fifth-grade classroom ranges from approximately second- to eighth-grade level. Therefore, if this book is to be read independently, it might be more appropriate for an average reader in the sixth grade.

Because all readers vary in ability, we recommend instructing students in proper self-selection techniques rather than labeling books along a difficulty scale. The Goldilocks rule (Taberski, 2000) is a useful tool with which to acquaint your students. This rule is based on the idea that there are three different types of texts in terms of difficulty: easy, just right, and challenging books. An easy text is one that the student can read with 95–100% accuracy and contains supportive text patterns, context clues, and illustrations. A just right book is read with 90–95% accuracy and contains some challenging words, but not so many that the student cannot read it. A challenging text is read with less than 90% accuracy and contains little support for the reader in terms of context clues, patterns, and so on. Providing minilessons for students can help acquaint them with the idea that they should select just right or easy books most of the time for independent reading.

The five-finger test can be used along with the Goldilocks rule to provide students with another measure of the difficulty of a book. With this technique, students select a page and count, using their fingers, the number of unknown words. If there are five or more unknown words, the book may be too difficult.

In addition to considering a book's difficulty, students should consider their own interest in the topic of the book, their prior knowledge about the book, and the extent to which the book is relevant to them. By teaching this concept, you can help your students select books that they are less likely to abandon quickly.

These techniques, like leveling systems, must be viewed with caution. Students with wide literary experiences, abiding interest in particular topics, or extensive background knowledge may bring far more to the literary experience than can be measured through a leveling system, readability formula, or five-finger test. Therefore, the use of such measures of difficulty must be tempered by your knowledge of individual students and their interests and experiences.

You may wonder whether to permit students to select library books well above or below their reading levels. Don't worry about it too much, but monitor students' library book selection to be sure it does not happen too often. Students who are highly motivated to read a particular book may successfully negotiate the book based on their interest alone. In the same way, students need opportunities to read "dessert" books, or "just for fun books" that may be easy for them. For this reason, students should be permitted to read outside their optimal reading zone on occasion.

By effectively organizing and managing the classroom library, you create a situation in which the library itself encourages the selection of appropriate and engaging books and makes those books accessible to students. Creating a library that is not only well organized but also enticing to students pays rich dividends in terms of helping students engage meaningfully with books.

Creating the Collection: Locating Materials

We are often asked how many books are needed for a good classroom library. Table 6 illustrates there is no readily agreed upon formula for an adequate number of books in a classroom library. This huge variance likely reflects the tension between the practical and the ideal.

We suggest that you work toward the recommendation from the International Reading Association (IRA): Seven books per student provides

Table 6. Recommendations for Number of Books in Classroom Libraries

Number of Books Per Student	Total Collection Size
• 7 (IRA, 1999) • 8 (Fractor et al., 1993) • 10–12 (Kelley & Clausen-Grace, 2007)	• 200–1000 plus (Routman, 2003) • 300–600 (Fountas & Pinnell, 2001) • 700–750 for primary grades and 400 for upper grades (Allington & Cunningham, 2007) • 1500–2000 (Reutzel & Fawson, 2002)

a strong basis for a good classroom library. This is both a reasonable and achievable goal. Moreover, we suggest having multiple copies of some books and enough books to cover a wide range of reading abilities so that students who struggle with reading or students who excel have access to appropriate books.

Obtaining books and materials inexpensively can seem to be a daunting task; however, there are a few ways to go about it, such as involving students in ordering books through Scholastic book clubs. Teachers get free books based on the number of books that students order, which can help build a library quickly. In addition, local Scholastic warehouses often have clearance sales, during which they sell quality paperback books for as little as $1 or $2.

Other excellent sources for inexpensive books include garage sales, public library book sales, and eBay. Websites such as www.bookcloseouts .com often have high-quality paperback books at inexpensive prices. Additional means for obtaining books involve holding book drives, where students bring in books from home; asking the PTA and other local businesses to donate funds for books; and asking parents to donate books to the classroom library on students' birthdays.

Another way to build the classroom library is to have students create their own books and reading materials. This can dramatically heighten student interest in reading and literacy. Brassell (1999), a former teacher in an urban California school with large numbers of ELLs, involved his students in creating their own Big Books, little books, magazines, bulletins, and newspapers written in Spanish. In a six-week period, they created more than 400 books, which they eagerly shared with one another and their families and friends. These books *became* Danny's classroom library. As a result of this project, the amount of student reading nearly doubled over the course of the school year.

Many experts recommend that classroom libraries include both a core collection, which stays in the classroom library, and a rotating collection, which comprises books from other sources such as the school media center or a public library. The rotating collection books only remain in the classroom library for a limited time, such as during a particular unit of study. If you have a limited number of books in your classroom collection, this can help provide more choices for students.

Creating the Collection: Selecting Materials

The process of selecting classroom library materials is not a simple one; it requires substantial thought and care. You must consider the instructional purposes, the needs and interests of the readers, the students' book preferences, and many other factors. According to Daniels (2004),

> As teachers build classroom libraries, they are trying to create something like the living room of a big, eclectically literate family, a place where all manner of fiction and nonfiction, books, magazines, clippings, articles, brochures, Web pages and newspapers surround us. Some of this material will pertain directly to the subjects that kids study in school, such as literature, history, science, and mathematics, while other parts of the collection can be deliciously random, chosen merely because they interest many, or some, or just a few young readers. (p. 1)

Effective book selection requires expertise in many areas, such as the following:

- Knowledge of children's literature, children's magazines and periodicals, and Internet resources, which necessitates reading widely in the various genres, thus developing familiarity with a wide range of books, authors, and websites

- The ability to evaluate literature and websites according to a variety of criteria

- Knowledge of students and their interests at various ages and stages of development, which helps you create a good fit between readers and books

Book selection is a continuing quest to locate those works that help students to develop a love for reading and to experience growth as readers. Much disagreement surrounds issues related to book selection for students. Children's book publishers produce more than 10,000 children's book each year (Bowker, 2000), ranging from those of excellent literary quality to those with mass appeal but minimal literary value. Should books be chosen on the basis of literary superiority, popularity with students, or some other criteria? How should you select classroom library books from among the thousands in print?

Reading reviews of trade books can provide guidance for selecting the best books for the classroom. Dozens of print resources, such as

Table 7. Online Children's Literature Resources

Webpage	Description
www.ala.org	The ALA provides a plethora of information on children's books, book awards, and other resources.
www.ala.org/booklinks	This section of the ALA website provides an online version of *Book Links*, a print periodical with thematic bibliographies of children's trade books, book reviews, author interviews, and other information on children's literature.
www.reading.org/Resources/Booklists/TeachersChoices.aspx	IRA's website features the IRA Choices booklists and other literature-related information.
www.cbcbooks.org	This website from the Children's Book Council contains interviews with authors, book recommendations, and much more.
www.socialstudies.com	The National Council for the Social Studies website provides links to social studies trade books for grades K–8.
www.nsta.org	This site from the National Science Teachers Association provides lesson plans and links to K–12 science trade books.
www.hbook.com	This online version of *The Horn Book* provides reviews of children's trade books, podcast interviews with authors, and blogs from children's literature experts.
bccb.lis.uiuc.edu	The online version of *The Bulletin of the Center for Children's Books* provides book reviews and annual lists of Blue Ribbon Winners, which are awarded annually by the staff of *The Bulletin*.

Book Links and *The Reading Teacher*, and online resources (see Table 7 for examples) are available to help you select books for your classroom. In addition, working collaboratively with the school librarian to identify quality titles can help identify books that work effectively in the classroom.

Book Selection Criteria

As teachers, we use literature and other materials to read aloud, teach students to identify literary elements, obtain information, promote writing, and much more. Classroom library books should help to further those curricular goals as well as provide books that appeal more specifically to student interests.

Students need to sample texts from different "registers." Such texts may range from more academic reading experiences to reading for sheer enjoyment. Children, like adults, apply different criteria for their own book selection depending upon their purpose. There may be times when they wish to read solely for entertainment or escape. During such times, they may read series books like the Magic Tree House Books or Harry Potter. On other occasions, they may read to fulfill their own curiosity. For example, when students complete a unit on the moon, some might choose to read Thimmesh's (2006) *Team Moon: How 400,000 People Landed Apollo 11 on the Moon* to satisfy their need to know more about this topic. Sometimes students read a book to enjoy a favorite story one more time. After *Because of Winn-Dixie* (DiCamillo, 2001) was read aloud to the class, some students may elect to read that book silently.

Thus, book and materials selection criteria are dynamic. They change with the goals and purposes of the reader. By maintaining a flexible approach to book selection and being exposed to a variety of reading materials both in and out of school, students have opportunities for meaningful encounters with print in a multiplicity of materials. This gives students a basis for comparing titles and seeing the difference between books of higher literary quality and those of lesser quality. Moreover, by providing students with opportunities for free—though properly managed—choice, we help to ensure that they choose reading for a leisure time activity.

A primary consideration in evaluating any children's book is literary quality. In fact, some experts believe that this should be the chief criterion for evaluating children's books (Lukens, 2005). Certainly, literary quality should be a consideration in evaluating every children's book, but it should not be an exclusive consideration. After all, there are many fine children's books that may not be of extremely high quality but do succeed in achieving other reading related goals and purposes for readers. The following sections delineate a few ways for determining a book's usefulness for the classroom.

Children's Classics. No classroom library would be complete without a selection of children's classics. Classics are those books that have stood the test of time and continue to attract readers from one generation to the next. These books not only demonstrate literary quality but also transmit the significant values of the culture. According to Kiefer, Hepler, and

Hickman (2006), the true classics of children's literature are those books that continue to be read by common consent, stating "No teacher or parent has to cajole a child into reading them" (p. 27).

What is the appeal of the classic children's book? Why do students return to these works year after year? First, these books generally possess magnificent stories. The compelling adventures they describe continue to intrigue today's students. Second, the characters, whether human or animal, are well drawn and memorable; Peter Pan, Alice, Jo March, Wilbur, and Charlotte live on in our minds long after childhood's end. Third, although these great books generally cross genre lines, many are fantasies that hold special appeal to students.

Award-Winning Books. Every intermediate and middle school classroom library should include a selection of Newbery Medal Books. The John Newbery Medal, named after the first English publisher of books intended expressly for children, is awarded for the most outstanding contribution to the field of U.S. children's literature in a given year and is the most prestigious award in the world for children's literature because it is based largely on the literary merit of the work. Some Newbery Medal winners, like *Holes* (Sachar, 1998) and *Number the Stars* (Lowry, 1989), achieve great popularity with students, although others do not. A brief list of popular Medal and Honor Books follows:

- *The Higher Power of Lucky* by Patron (2006)
- *Rules* by Lord (2006)
- *The Tale of Despereaux* by DiCamillo (2004)
- *The Watsons Go to Birmingham—1963* by Curtis (1995)
- *Shiloh* by Naylor (1991)
- *Maniac Magee* by Spinelli (1993)

The Caldecott Medal is awarded annually to the illustrator of the most distinguished picture book published in the United States, in commemoration of the great English illustrator Randolph Caldecott. This award not only is given for excellence in artwork but also requires that the text of the book work synergistically with the illustrations. Caldecott Medal winners are typically suitable for younger students, but some such as Selznick's (2007) *The Invention of Hugo Cabret* are clearly better suited for upper elementary and middle school students. Some popular Caldecott Medal and Honor Books include the following:

- *Kitten's First Full Moon* written and illustrated by Henkes (2004)
- *What Do You Do With a Tail Like This?* written and illustrated by Jenkins and Page (2003)
- *The Three Pigs* written and illustrated by Wiesner (2001)
- *Click, Clack, Moo: Cows That Type* written by Cronin (2000)
- *The Paperboy* written and illustrated by Pilkey (1996)
- *Tar Beach* written and illustrated by Ringgold (1991)

Some teachers and librarians limit their selections to Newbery Medal and Caldecott Medal books, but there are many problems inherent in such an approach. Because of the difficulty level of these award-winning books, many may be beyond the reading ability of elementary students. Also, although many outstanding books have received the award, other highly praised works, such as *Charlotte's Web* (White, 1952), have not. Limiting students' reading choices to Newbery books prevents exposure to many other outstanding books; it also limits exposure to genres such as nonfiction and poetry, because few Newbery winners fall into these categories. Furthermore, not all Newbery Medal books are popular with students. Lacy (1980) suggests the Newbery Honor Books offer greater potential for popularity with students than the award-winning books themselves.

While the Newbery and Caldecott Medals are the best-known book awards, dozens of other awards provide teachers with lists of high-quality, library-appropriate books. These awards recognize books on the basis of a variety of criteria. The Coretta Scott King Award, for example, is given for the most outstanding contribution by an African American author; the Orbis Pictus Award is given for the most outstanding nonfiction book of the year. All of these awards recognize books of high literary quality that represent the best books available for students today. Some well-known children's book awards include the following:

- The ALA Annual List of Notable Books
- The Laura Ingalls Wilder Award
- The Boston Globe–Horn Book Award

- The Notable Books for a Global Society
- The Tomás Rivera Mexican American Children's Book Award

Booklists. The Children's Choices booklist can provide teachers with a rich resource for determining students' reading preferences. This list, which is cosponsored by the IRA and the Children's Book Council, represents books selected by children for children. As part of the Children's Choices project, more than 10,000 children around the United States vote on their favorite books. The Children's Choices lists provide many excellent book titles for reluctant readers. For example, the Children's Choices books for 2007 include humorous titles such as *The Secret Science Project That Ate the School* (Sierra, 2006) and *Burger Boy* (Durant, 2006), a story about a boy who eats so many burgers that he turns into one. Books for older readers included *Bunnicula Meets Edgar Alan Crow* (Howe, 2006) and nonfiction titles such as *Friends: Making Them and Keeping Them* (Criswell, 2006). Additional Children's Choices books that are sure to captivate the reluctant reader include the following:

- *Fairytale News* by Hawkins and Hawkins (2005)
- *Knuffle Bunny: A Cautionary Tale* by Willems (2004)
- *Dogs: How to Choose and Care for a Dog* by Jeffrey (2004)
- *Great White Sharks* by Markle (2004)
- *What If You Met a Pirate: A Historical Voyage of Seafaring Speculation* by Adkins (2004)
- *Halloween Crafts* by Robinson (2004)
- *There Once Was a Very Odd School and Other Lunch-Box Limericks* by Krensky (2004)

Another booklist, published annually in IRA's journal *The Reading Teacher*, is the Teachers' Choices, which features books that are actually piloted in elementary classrooms and then recommended by the teachers involved in the project.

The Notable Children's Books in the Language Arts is another popular list; it is published annually in both the *Journal of Children's Literature* and *Language Arts*. Likewise, the Notable Children's Trade Books in the Field of Social Studies is published each year in *Social Education*, and the Outstanding Science Trade Books for Students is published in the March issue of *Science & Children*. These lists can help you add quality social studies and science trade books to your collections.

Selecting Diverse Genres

Lists of classics, award winners, and recommended books can guide you and your students toward books of excellence. However, when these books are used to the exclusion of other works, students are exposed to an extremely limited view of our world and the people who inhabit it. The variety of genres available in today's trade books offers a vast array of titles from which to choose, ranging from easy-to-read titles using engaging formats to extremely sophisticated treatments of complex topics. The greatest challenge is deciding which books to choose from the enormous possibilities available. Books selected for the classroom library should not duplicate those in the school library but rather should be tailored specifically to the wants and needs of your own students. The following sections describe just a few of the genres the classroom library should include.

Picture Books. No classroom library is complete without picture books. And every genre is represented in today's picture books. The stunning visual quality of today's picture books make them indispensable resources for engaging students at all grade levels. At the primary level, for example, books like *Lilly's Purple Plastic Purse* (Henkes, 1996) make ideal read-alouds. Picture books contribute to the curriculum in myriad ways at the upper levels as well, such as picture book biographies *Leonardo da Vinci* (Stanley, 1996) or *Michelangelo* (Stanley, 2000), which contain incredible paintings representative of the styles of these artists. Humorous picture books like *Detective LaRue: Letters From the Investigation* (Teague, 2004) stretch the boundaries of the picture book format while they amuse and intrigue students.

Fiction. Classroom library researchers have noted that fiction usually dominates classroom collections (Duke, 2000; Stead, 2002). Books in fantasy, historical fiction, and realistic fiction genres are perennially popular with students and form an important part of a classroom library collection. We believe fiction deserves its share of attention in every classroom library; however, researchers have noted three major problems with fiction-dominant collections. First and most obvious, students are denied access to the poetry, biography, and information books that often have great appeal.

Second, these collections often feature books that are too difficult for students to read. For instance, Martinez, Roser, Worthy, Strecker, and Gough (1997) found that the proportion of lower level books in classroom libraries was smaller than the relative demand for those books. Reading suffers when students have a steady diet of books that are too hard for them (Allington, 2009b; Routman, 1999). Given the ever-increasing range of reading levels, it is crucial that students have access to books available from a wide range of levels on the same themes and topics (Biancarosa & Snow, 2004; Gambrell & Mazzoni, 1999). By creating thematic collections, you can provide opportunities for students to read different books and still contribute to class discussions.

Third, the fiction books you choose sometimes lack appeal and relevance to students. Worthy, Broaddus, and Ivey (2001) note that teachers often select books of high literary quality for their students. Yet students often prefer humorous, scary, and series books to the books available to them (Worthy, Moorman, & Turner, 1999). Obviously, it is important to include both books of interest and books of high literary quality in your classroom library.

Poetry. Poetry should play a prominent role in every classroom library. Poetry is often featured on standardized tests, so students need opportunities to regularly read, write, and respond to poetry across grade levels (Young, 2006a). Today's poetry books are incredibly varied in content, ranging from humorous titles like *Scien-Trickery: Riddles in Science* (Lewis, 2007) to biographical verse such as *Carver: A Life in Poems* (Nelson, 2001) or *Twelve Rounds to Glory: The Story of Muhammad Ali* (Smith, 2007) to poems for multiple voices like *Big Talk: Poems for Four Voices* (Fleischman, 2000). Many researchers also note that poetry is a powerful tool for introducing and extending content area subjects (Hadaway, Vardell, & Young, 2002; Vardell, Hadaway, & Young, 2002). Even more important, many students thrive on this genre because of its brevity, rhythm, and accessibility.

Nonfiction. Many students enjoy reading about real-world topics. Nonfiction trade books address a range of topics from ants to zeppelins.

These books connect students with real people and places from the present and past. Nonfiction books often contain stunning color photography, primary source documents, and other factual media. They complement content learning in virtually every subject area. In fact, the 2008 Newbery Medal book, *Good Masters! Sweet Ladies! Voices From a Medieval Village* (Schlitz, 2007), was written by a teacher whose students were studying the Middle Ages. It consists of a series of 22 dramatic monologues about the residents of a medieval village and combines poetry, historical fiction, and nonfiction to provide a fascinating glimpse of medieval life through the eyes of young people.

Nonfiction trade books also provide a rich resource for student research. As students engage in inquiry projects designed to answer their own questions about a topic, they have access to a range of resources beyond just the encyclopedia from which to mine information. These resources provide information on different facets of a topic at a variety of difficulty levels, allowing *all* students to engage with information in meaningful ways. Consider, for example, a fourth-grade student conducting an inquiry on snakes. To obtain a broad survey of the topic, the student can consult titles like *Amazing Snakes* (Parsons, 1990), *Snakes* (Gibbons, 2007), or *Slinky, Scaly, Slithery Snakes* (Patent, 2003).

More narrowly focused books provide even more specialized information. To explore the care and feeding of pet snakes, Gutman's (2001) engaging *Becoming Best Friends With Your Iguana, Snake, or Turtle* is an ideal resource. A more challenging title, Montgomery's (1999) *The Snake Scientist*, with amazing photographs by Nic Bishop, introduces students to the work of a zoologist who studies snake behavior. Dewey's (2000) *Rattlesnake Dance: True Tales, Mysteries, and Rattlesnake Ceremonies* provides a personal account of the author's close encounters with these reptiles, starting with the time she was bitten by a rattlesnake at the age of 9. Maintaining a sizable body of such works in your classroom library allows you the opportunity to model the uses of such books for inquiry study and helps students understand the different types of information provided by each book type.

Helping Students to Select Diverse Genres

In order to become successful readers, students need exposure to a variety of genres. In many, if not most, classrooms that access is largely defined by state-adopted basal readers that have traditionally provided students with exposure to a narrow range of text types (Moss, 2008). According to Palincsar and Duke (2004), educators need to expose students to those text types they want them to learn to read and write.

Genre wheels can help students experience diverse genres and can help you engage your students in selecting books from each literary genre. To make a genre wheel, create a circle out of heavy paper and divide it into eight sections—poetry, informational, science fiction/fantasy, mystery, biography, folklore, realistic fiction, and historical fiction—and insert a spinner. Each of the eight sections can be colored. Students use the spinner to determine the color-coded genre they will read. Using an incentive chart, students can place a sticky dot next to their name in the color representative of the book's genre.

A second form of genre wheel involves giving each student a genre wheel handout that they maintain in their reading folders. Students color each genre as they complete books within that text type.

The genre passport is still another means for recording books read according to genre. As students complete books and contract activities for each genre, they record the book titles in their passports according to genre. Once the students complete all their activities for each book, they receive a stamp in the passport for the designated genre.

Creating the Collection: Considering Students' Reading Interests

Many U.S. students choose not to read. As stated in Chapter 1, interest in reading typically declines in the upper elementary grades and continues its descent through the high school years. According to Thomas and Moorman (1983), "The student who can read but chooses not to is probably the most crucial concern confronting our educational institutions today. It is not illiteracy we are combating, but aliteracy" (p. 137). Because time spent reading is associated with competence in reading, students who do not read often lose ground academically even if they were not initially struggling readers (Mullis, et al., 1993; Stanovich, 1986).

This decline in interest in reading may have much to do with the kinds of reading materials and experiences students encounter in school. According to Worthy and colleagues (1999), there is an ever-increasing gap between student reading preferences and the materials schools provide. Their research with middle graders demonstrates the importance of providing students with books and materials they want to read. It is impossible to underestimate the importance of interest to reading. Interest motivates students to read, prompts them to read more difficult material, and can result in more time spent reading (Kragler & Nolley, 1996).

How do those books chosen by students compare with those identified by adults as books students should read? Lehman (1991) found that (a) substantial differences do exist between award-winning books students prefer and those they do not, (b) students prefer predictable qualities, optimistic tone, and a lively pace, and (c) students prefer action-oriented structures and complete plot resolutions.

Identifying Student Reading Interests

Students' preferences for certain kinds of books not only should be honored but also should form an important basis for classroom library book selection. How can you determine individual students' interests? Three techniques can help achieve this goal. First, observe students as they participate in various classroom activities and note and record areas of interest identified during class assignments, oral discussions, group projects, and so on. Second, initiate informal discussions with students, parents, peers, and others to help identify areas of interest. During parent conferences or open houses, ask about students' interests and out-of-school activities. Third, use interest inventories, which can take a variety of forms such as favorite booklists, responses to questions through a multiple-choice format, or a questionnaire, as shown in Figure 1. The interest inventory might also become an interview that you conduct with your students early in the year to learn about their interests.

By learning about student interests, we can guide students to select books from the classroom library that will allow them to become engaged readers, or readers who read a significant amount of text. In addition, by matching students with books that engage them, they develop the reading stamina necessary for the types of complex reading experiences they will encounter as they move into middle school and high school.

Figure 1. Reading Interest Survey

1. What do you like to do outside of school?_____
2. What activities do you do outside of school (clubs, sports, lessons)? _____
   _____
3. What is your favorite school subject and why? _____
4. What do you want to be when you grow up? _____
5. What would you like to learn about this year?_____
6. What is your favorite book? Why is it your favorite?_____
   _____
   _____
7. Which person would you like to read about?_____
8. What kinds of books do you enjoy the most? _____
9. Do you read at home? What kinds of things do you read? _____
10. Would you like to read about any of the topics or kinds of books below? Please circle
    the ones that sound interesting to you.

Animals	Funny stories	Science
Fairy tales	Picture books	Historical stories
People your age	Poetry	History
Famous people	Mysteries	Math
Adventure stories	Music	Health
Fantasy	Art	Scary stories

What Research Says About Reading Interests

Studies of students' reading interests can provide important information about the kinds of books and topics that students like to read. The role of reading interest is a powerful one; interest in particular texts can mean the difference between a student who persists at reading and one who gives up quickly. While every student is different, these studies provide some general guidelines for book selection based on specific book characteristics. A working knowledge of topics that interest students can help light the spark that may turn a reluctant reader into a ravenous one.

However, students' book tastes are individual. Though studies suggest middle graders love adventure stories, the sixth grader sitting before you may dislike adventure stories but also may be passionately interested in nonfiction books about birds. We cannot generalize about students' book preferences any more than we can generalize about what a particular adult will enjoy. Factors including age, gender, home environment, teacher, classroom environment, accessibility of books, and academic ability all help to determine students' reading interests.

Although content is typically regarded as the most important criterion students use in selecting books, physical appearance of books is important as well. Students of all ages select books based on type size, style, length, illustrations, and covers (Kiefer et al., 2006). Illustrations are important to students' choices at all grade levels (Kiefer et al., 2006). Upper elementary students often enjoy nonfiction books with maps, photos, and other visual features (Moss & Hendershot, 2002).

Furthermore, students enjoy books with characters who have experiences similar to their own (Rinehart, Gerlach, Wisell, & Welker, 1998). They select books with characters of their own age and gender (Harkrader & Moore, 1997), and they tend to enjoy books with fast-paced plots.

In terms of topics and types, students of all ages enjoy books about animals, humor, action, suspense, and surprise (Keifer et al., 2006); however, students' book preferences undergo radical changes as they progress from the elementary to the upper elementary grades (Donovan, Smolkin, & Lomax, 2000; Hickman, 1982).

Younger students typically enjoy folk-tales and fantasy (Moss & McDonald, 2004), informational texts (Caswell & Duke, 1998; Kletzien, 1998), humorous books (Doiron, 2003), and poetry, particularly with rhyme or humor (Monson & Sebesta, 1991). Upper elementary students generally express preferences for humor and poetry, as well as realistic fiction, adventures, mysteries, and fantasy (Boraks, Hoffman, & Bauer, 1997).

After the age of 9, students' reading interests tend to diverge along gender lines. Upper elementary level boys typically enjoy adventure books (Rinehart et al., 1998), science books, and animal books including topics like reptiles and dinosaurs. Boys often express interest in nonfiction topics such as sports, machines, and vehicles and appear to read more nonfiction than girls (Boraks et al., 1997; Doiron, 2003). Conversely girls generally prefer fiction (Asselin, 2003), particularly romance books (Rinehart et al., 1998) and express interests in books about family, home life, or friends (Doiron, 2003). Girls seem to enjoy reading about familiar life issues, but their interests also extend to animals (Doiron, 2003) and poetry (Greenlaw & Wielan, 1979).

Books for Boys. During the past few years, experts have become concerned about studies indicating that boys read less proficiently than girls and experience a higher incidence of school failure (Ross, McKechnie, & Rothbauer, 2006). One response to media attention to this issue was popular author Jon Scieszka's "Guys Read" (www.guysread.com), an engaging website that focuses on books with particular appeal to boys. Books like *Don't Let the Pigeon Drive the Bus!* (Willems, 2003) and *The Dangerous Book for Boys* (Iggulden & Iggulden, 2007) appeal to younger and older male readers, respectively. *Great Books for Boys: More than 600 Books for Boys 2 to 14* (Odean, 1998) is an excellent resource for teachers and librarians.

Books for Girls. In the same way, it is important to provide books that appeal specifically to girls. More and more books cater specifically to female audiences, particularly at the upper elementary level. Titles like *Girls Think of Everything: Stories of Ingenious Inventions by Women* (Thimmesh, 2000) and *The Girls' Book: How to Be the Best at Everything* (Foster, 2007) are representative of the increasingly popular genre of "girl power" books. *Great Books for Girls: More Than 600 Books to Inspire Today's Girls and Tomorrow's Women* (Odean, 1997) can help teachers and librarians locate titles designed to appeal specifically to girls.

Books for ELLs. ELLs may find multicultural books that depict their home language and customs to be of particular interest. For example, English–Spanish titles like *A Gift From Papá Diego* (Sáenz, 1998), which accurately depicts specific customs related to the Mexican culture, might be particularly appropriate for Mexican American students. It is important to provide students with books in their home language whenever possible because "developing literacy in the primary language is an extremely efficient means of developing literacy in the second language. To become good readers in the primary language, however, children need to read in the primary language" (Krashen, 1997, pp. 20–21).

Remember, however, that the maturity, backgrounds (family, cultural, language, and knowledge), and interests of ELLs vary tremendously from totally non–English-speaking immigrants or refugees to native-born students who have a general knowledge of English. For this reason, ELLs need access to a broad range of titles at varying reading levels. Many ELLs benefit from the visual element provided by graphic novels. ELLs also benefit from picture dictionaries with illustrations and labels (Jobe & Dayton-Sakari, 1999). These books are helpful tools for both building vocabulary and for writing when students need to find the English label for a concept known in their home language.

Books All Students Enjoy. In this section, we try to give particular attention to reading materials that might be attractive to those students who finding reading difficult. Many of these students enjoy series books or television/movie tie-ins such as the A Series of Unfortunate Events (Snicket, 2002–2006) books. Students often enjoy joke and riddle books, humorous books, and books about media celebrities. Comic literature and graphic novels enjoy enormous popularity with today's students; these titles are increasing in quantity and quality every day.

Series books such as the Magic Tree House books (Osborne, 1992–2010) and the Captain Underpants books (Pilkey, 1997–2006) are perennial favorites with students. See Table 8 for a list of series books appropriate for elementary students. These books often possess predictable language, action, and characters. This predictability, coupled with the replication of characters across the various books, provides a familiarity students often enjoy. Also, students identify readily with the characters in these books. They feel as though they "know" these characters; they don't have to become acquainted with a new set of characters with each book. Furthermore, they become comfortable with the consistent format that these books provide.

Table 8. Series Books for Elementary Students

Primary	Intermediate
• Amelia Bedelia	• American Girls
• Captain Underpants	• Bone
• Clifford the Big Red Dog	• Boxcar Children
• Curious George	• Diary of a Wimpy Kid
• Geronimo Stilton	• Little House on the Prairie
• Junie B. Jones	• A Series of Unfortunate Events
• Magic Tree House	• The Time Warp Trio

Graphic Novels. Today's graphic novels provide a unique form of reading for today's students. Books that combine the visual with the verbal in new ways are one of the most important trends in literature today, and the motivational power of these titles is significant. The unique format of books like *The Invention of Hugo Cabret* (Selznick, 2007), which uses movielike illustrations that help to advance the story in place of text, is an exemplar of the changing forms of books. Graphic novels such as the popular Bone series (Smith, 1991–2004), *Babymouse: Beach Babe* (Holm, 2006), and the many available manga titles provide motivating reading for reluctant readers of all ages. Although these books may lack the literary quality of a classic book, they have value for young readers and provide a bridge to more sophisticated reading. In addition, they add to the reservoir of student reading experiences, and the richer this reservoir of experiences and ideas, the more effective students' transactions with literature become over time (Purves & Monson, 1984). For more popular graphic novel suggestions, see Table 9.

Magazines. Magazines are favorite reading for many children and adults. Children's magazines such as *Discovery Girls, Kids Discover, National Geographic Kids, Ranger Rick,* and *Sports Illustrated for Kids* make good additions to the classroom library. Magazines create opportunities for those students who enjoy reading shorter texts that they can complete in one sitting.

Table 9. Graphic Novels for Elementary Students

Primary	Intermediate
• *Amelia Earhart: Free in the Skies* (Burleigh, 2003)	• *Amelia Rules! The Whole World's Crazy* (Gownley, 2009)
• *Benny and Penny: Just Pretend* (Hayes, 2008)	• *Artemis Fowl: The Graphic Novel* (Colfer & Donkin, 2007)
• *Camp Babymouse* (Holm, 2007)	• *To Dance: A Ballerina's Graphic Novel* (Siegel, 2006)
• *The Princess and the Frog* (Eisner, 2003)	• *Hercules: The 12 Labors* (Storrie, 2007)
• *Shrek* (Evanier, Bachs, & Fernandez, 2004)	• *Jellaby* (Soo, 2008)

Multicultural Books. Quality multicultural books provide both a window and a mirror (Bishop, 1990). They let today's diverse student populations see into other cultures as well as see themselves in books. Virtually all groups are represented in today's multicultural literature, including Latinos, Africans and African Americans, Asians and Asian Americans, and so on. Positive and accurate portrayals of members of parallel cultures are essential. In addition to evaluating such books for literary quality, you should ensure that books chosen for the classroom library (a) provide diversity and range of representation, (b) avoid stereotyping, (c) use appropriate language, and (d) contain appropriate cultural perspectives (Kiefer et al., 2006). To provide diversity and range of representation, books selected must portray members of parallel cultures in a wide variety of economic circumstances, lifestyles, occupations, and so on. Customs and values of each group should be accurately portrayed. Illustrations should capture the distinctive characteristics of a particular group and should portray scenes containing members of many cultures. By consistently portraying Asian Americans as studious scientists or engineers, for example, we reinforce a stereotype just as damaging and inaccurate as portraying Hispanics as poor migrant workers. Members of particular cultural groups must be regarded as unique individuals with their own values, beliefs, and opinions, not as monolithic.

The importance of a classroom library cannot be taken lightly. As Ramos and Krashen (1998) state,

> Providing interesting books for children is a powerful incentive for reading, perhaps the most powerful incentive possible. This conclusion is consistent with research showing that extrinsic incentives for reading have not been successful, while improving access to books has been successful in encouraging reading. (p. 614)

Bernhardt (2000) further substantiates the value of literature-based learning opportunities for ELLs in her synthesis of second-language reading research: "Providing students extended reading experiences over time with authentic, not grammatically sequenced or altered, texts promoted the greatest gains in comprehension over time" (p. 800).

Students' reading engagement plays a key role in their academic success. Both comprehension and achievement improve when students increase their reading volume (Allington, 2006). Classroom libraries have the potential to increase students' access to books and to stimulate their desire to read, which is, after all, the point of teaching students how to read.

A DISCUSSION WITH TONY STEAD

Tony Stead is an Australian educator and consultant who works with teachers across Australia, Canada, and the United States. His most recent book is *Good Choice! Supporting Independent Reading and Response K–6* (2009).

Terrell Young: How have you seen interest in classroom libraries change in the past 10 years?

Tony Stead: There was more emphasis on classroom libraries 10 years ago; that interest has waned over the past 5 years. Independent reading has taken a back burner. Since then, the emphasis on leveled text and core reading programs has dominated in [United States] classrooms. In many classrooms, I've observed that independent reading had been relegated as a center activity. When the only independent reading is during center time, kids are not spending enough time reading and are not benefiting from teacher monitoring and support. Sadly, there was definitely a period where not a lot of districts were viewing independent reading as a focused part of their literacy instruction. Now there seems to be a greater interest in independent reading and classroom libraries.

TY: Why are classroom libraries so important to independent reading?

TS: During reading aloud, shared reading, and guided reading it is the teacher who selects text. When do children select their own text? That is the goal of any good program. Classroom libraries are critically important so kids can learn to make book selections. Kids need to know how to use their own interests to guide their book choices. The classroom library is the heartbeat of the classroom. *Every* classroom needs a library. We look at a builder and see that wood and nails are prime materials for his craft; for kids learning to read the classroom library provides them with what they need to turn them into readers. A love of literature is essential to get kids to want to read.

TY: What are your greatest concerns with the classroom libraries you see when you walk into classrooms?

TS: Oh, there are so many! Often they are just thrown together. Many teachers do not know how to use them or set them up. I've noticed that attractive, well-organized libraries are more likely to be found in K–2 classrooms.

Kids often have no input in the organization and monitoring of the classroom collection. To make a difference for kids and their reading, the classroom library should belong to students, *not* the teacher.

Many teachers do not know how to set them up. Most are concerned about leveled texts, or how to distinguish between fiction and nonfiction. Teachers are often searching for the one best way to organize their classroom book collection. There is no one single way. Every classroom library should not look the same. The interests of the learners are paramount. I always start the year with a survey to learn of their interests. In my book, I illustrate how even kindergartens can draw pictures of what interests them. As teachers, we need to respond to our students' interests. Sometimes we find our kids are stuck in a groove, and we need to find ways to help them so they read more broadly.

TY: What is the best advice you have for teachers regarding classroom libraries and independent reading?

TS: Establish a time when students are engaged in independent reading. Setting that time and routine up is number one. This regularly scheduled time allows children to develop reading stamina and to see reading as a pleasurable and important part of their lives.

Look at what is available in the classroom library. Don't try to set up the whole thing the first three weeks of school. Most teachers want to get it set up and done rather than seeing the library being an ongoing project. Student involvement in the organization of the classroom library is key to its success. We need to remember that kids get overwhelmed when there is too much material available. It is too much when there is a sea of spines facing them. It is an overload when a child encounters 60 books on space. He will spend more time looking for a book than actually reading. Kids often just pick anything without considering their interest and purpose for reading. They need our help to make good choices.

Start by finding students' outside interests. Too often teachers only consider books for their libraries and overlook the wonderful potential of magazines. We need to remember that when kids select a novel to read, it is a huge investment of their time. That is where the importance of nonfiction comes into play. As we read magazines and newspapers, we can copy great articles that will appeal to our students. These can be laminated and added to the classroom library so kids can browse through them at their leisure and when they are not ready to commit to reading an entire book.

Kids need to learn to make their own selections. Independent reading is about reading what children *want* to read rather than only reading books at or just below their level. Books they have read during guided reading are another great source of independent reading materials. Independent reading is for many purposes, and kids need a range of selections for those purposes—browsing, pleasure, research, support to content understanding, and a springboard for writing.

In the end, I want kids to have a wide selection of books and be able to read different things for different purposes. The entire class may read selections on space because that is the topic for science, but they should also have books available for their own pleasure as well.

By grade 6, kids stop reading for pleasure because of the overload of assigned reading. They often feel tired of reading and spend lots of time on [video games] and the computer. I had this concern about my own son, but I was delighted when he became a voracious reader again during holidays. Having the privilege of reading for pleasure becomes lost when kids have so many things to do with what they have read. Twelve- and 13-year-olds rarely read books, and fewer books are sold for that age range. The key is to get kids off the computer and back to books so we do not lose them completely.

TY: What is your best advice for choosing books for the classroom library?

TS: Many teachers complain that there are no funds for buying books so I always make a big push to find interesting articles online or in magazines and put them on cardboard so kids can read them. As a firm believer in the power of the reading–writing connection, I always encourage adding kids-authored selections so they can read their own buddy's publications as well as those by published authors. Writers cannot write above what they read so that is a great way to think about leveling. Those are also some of the most popular books in the room; kids love borrowing other student-written books to read.

TY: What are your recommendations regarding a balance between trade books and leveled text in classroom libraries?

TS: First and foremost, the classroom library needs to offer students a variety of reading materials. It is great to have leveled texts if all of the books are not leveled. Yet, at the beginning of the year in a grade 1 classroom, the teacher will need books at the Fountas and Pinnell C, D, E, F, and G levels. There are far too many classrooms where we just have kids selecting books by level. We forget the role of interest and background knowledge. I'm frustrated when I go in classrooms where I hear a child say, "I can't read that book because I'm only a D." I quickly respond, "You are not a D, you are a reader!"

Organization of the books should be by topic first and the leveling is secondary. Our goal is to organize the books in such a way as to help kids make wise decisions. No more than 30% have a leveled coding. For instance, in a section of books about space there should be a range of levels with some of the books marked with stickers to give kids guidance. The ultimate goal is that by grade 3 or 4 there would be no leveling at all. Kids cannot make good choices until they become fluent readers. Kids often choose books that are either too hard or those that they have read 100 times. That is where the conference comes into play.

TY: After the National Reading Panel report, many people have suggested that independent reading should take place outside of school. What is your response to that suggestion?

TS: Frankly, I couldn't disagree with this more. We simply cannot rely on home reading. The ones who read a lot do, but others do not. Children go off into their rooms and then parents are signing forms indicating they have read but not monitoring their kids' reading. The purpose of reading is so kids will take independent reading into their own lives. If we cannot get kids to enjoy reading, then we have failed them. One of my favorite quotes is by Mark Twain who said, "The man who does not read good books has no advantage over the man who cannot read them." I believe that we have failed kids if we do not nurture in them a love of reading.

I believe that there should be at least 20 minutes of independent reading where the teachers monitor students in their book selections and help them learn to make good choices. The conference is a time for the teacher to monitor, to help, to nudge, and to push. The teacher role is pivotal during that time.

TY: What do you view as the role of instruction during independent reading time?

TS: Instruction should involve teacher monitoring to ensure that kids have text that they can and want to read. We need to extend their reading repertoire to help them read widely and deeply. In many classrooms, the girls are the strongest readers, but they rarely read nonfiction. Thus, in conferences I try to encourage nonfiction reading: "Allison, I notice you are reading lots of Judy Blume books. That's great! We all have our favorite authors and want to read all of their books. I notice you are interested in horses on your survey. Here is a book I like that I think you would enjoy. Would you add it to your book bag and see if you like it?" The emphasis is on reading widely. Girls often fall into narrative and rarely read nonfiction. Some girls think being good in science and math is a boy thing, and we have to break that notion.

With boys, I try to introduce novels and short stories to break their nonfiction-only habit. There once was a void in good fiction books for boys. There are more quality books available for them now. Boys get caught up into just one type of fiction reading so teachers need to work to extend their repertoire. I often read aloud just the first chapter of a good book to hook the boys. Then I have three copies of the book available in the classroom library. I've found this to be a great way to hook boys on particular fiction books.

The best way to promote books is by letting kids organize the classroom library. One third-grade teacher I know accomplished this by dividing her kids into partners with one being the seeker and the other a keeper. Each pair had a topic such as mysteries or frogs. She placed all the books in the middle of the room, and the seeker would find all the books on their topic and bring them to the keeper. The keeper would make sure the books really belong in the tub for their topic. It is a wonderful way to get kids to know what is available in the classroom collection.

I believe teachers should share the new books for the classroom library and have the kids remind them of where they should be placed. "Here's a book on tarantulas and here's another on Egypt. Where should we put them?"

I am a great believer that the teacher read-aloud book is sought after by every child. I always recommend that teachers have at least two copies so kids can read the second copy in "our favorite read-aloud" tub. Likewise, I never buy a popular book unless I can have six copies for the classroom library so kids can select them to read during independent reading time.

CHAPTER 3

Structuring Independent Reading Experiences

A s we discussed in Chapter 1, the face of classroom independent reading time is changing. Because the effectiveness of SSR is being questioned, new models of independent reading are taking its place. Described variously as scaffolded silent reading (Reutzel et al., 2008), structured independent reading (Fountas & Pinnell, 2001), or R^5 (read, relax, reflect, respond, rap; Kelley & Clausen-Grace, 2006), all of these models are predicated on the premise that both students and teachers should do more than just read during independent reading time.

Reutzel, Fawson, and Smith (2008) developed scaffolded silent reading as an alternative to traditional SSR. Scaffolded silent reading incorporates research-based practices associated with improved reading achievement including teacher guidance, structure, and accountability so that students can transfer oral reading skills to effective silent independent reading. Using this model, you would teach book selection strategies, guide student book choices, monitor student reading during individual reading conferences, and hold students accountable for reading across genres and completing response projects.

Reutzel, Fawson, and Smith (2008) conducted a yearlong controlled experiment that compared the effectiveness of this model with guided repeated oral reading with feedback, which was the NRP's (NICHD, 2000) recommended form of reading practice. The study, which involved 4 classrooms, 4 third-grade teachers, and 72 students, showed that scaffolded silent reading was as effective as guided repeated oral reading in developing reading accuracy, rate, expression and comprehension.

In this chapter, we describe a model for structuring independent reading experiences in ways that, like the scaffolded silent reading model, incorporate structure, accountability, and teacher feedback. Providing time for practice of reading skills through pleasure reading is a central focus of our independent reading model. This sustained practice builds reading stamina—a crucial need for students, whether they are reading a book or a standardized test selection. In this model, students are accountable for their reading through conferences with you, record-keeping, goal setting, and responses to texts. You, too, are accountable for (a) teaching students about procedures, processes, and skills, (b) helping students set appropriate reading goals, and (c) monitoring and assessing student's progress toward their identified goals through conferences.

Key Components of an Independent Reading Program

Because independent reading time provides an important opportunity for reading practice, it should not occur as the occasional add-on but rather as an integral part of a balanced reading program. We recommend that an independent reading program have two components: 20 minutes of community reading time at least twice a week and 60 minutes devoted to supported independent reading time (SIRT) every day. In the following sections, we discuss each of these components in detail in terms of scheduling, activities, and record keeping (see Table 10).

Community Reading Time

The best time for your 20 minutes of community reading time depends upon your classroom schedule. You might schedule this time at the beginning of the school day, before or after lunch, or just before SIRT. A community of readers develops in classrooms in which students read

Table 10. Components of an Independent Reading Program

Component	Community Reading Time	Supported Independent Reading Time (SIRT)
Schedule	20 minutes twice weekly	60 minutes daily
Activities	• Book talks • Interactive read-alouds • Book sharing • Time for reading	• Focus lessons (procedural and literacy strategies) • Time for reading • Student–teacher conferences • Response to reading
Record keeping		

regularly (Hepler & Hickman, 1982). Students in such classrooms not only read recommended books but also motivate one another to read by suggesting books to one another; they use the classroom community to enhance their own literacy. Discussion within the community also helps students pick up "reader behaviors" that tell them how readers act. For example, students see that readers enjoy reading books and seek out more books to read.

The development of a community of readers is essential to a successful independent reading program. This feeling of community around books and reading helps students select books they want to read, familiarizes them with the books available in the classroom, and creates independence in terms of book selection.

Community reading time should include the following four motivation-building activities: book talks, teacher interactive read-aloud, time for reading, and book sharing. Not all of these activities may occur every day, but they should comprise the content of the 20-minute community reading time block regularly. Formal assessment is not part of this time, but informal assessment of student attitudes and motivation for reading should be ongoing.

Book Talks. During the first five minutes of community reading time, book talks can introduce students to books, magazine articles, websites, and other print or electronic materials from the school or classroom library. You can give book talks any time; as students learn about the process, they can begin book talking for their peers. The purpose of a book talk is to generate enthusiasm for a book. It should not involve a dull recitation of the entire plot of the book but rather be a three- to five-minute book commercial that includes the title of the book, the author, and a brief mention of the characters and plot. Often a book talk involves reading a short section from the book to heighten interest. Book talks can take several interesting forms:

- Cliffhangers—Summarize the plot to a certain, dramatic point and then stop, leaving the outcome a surprise.

- Character based—Describe one of the characters in the book or pretend to be that character and tell the story from the character's point of view. You can also present this as an interview with the main character. Props and costumes can contribute to student understanding of the character.

- First sentences—Collect a variety of books with intriguing first sentences and present these sentences to students as teasers for the entire book.

- Grab bag—Locate small objects that represent different books and put them into a bag. Have students pull a random object from the bag and then book talk each one. These objects should provide a visual cue for the book to be described. For example, a small pair of round glasses could represent *Harry Potter and the Sorcerer's Stone* (Rowling, 1998).

- Ten questions—Hold up a nonfiction book and allow the students to ask 10 questions that they think will be answered in the book. Tell the students whether they were correct.

- Readers Theatre teaser—Have a few students dramatically read to the class a Readers Theatre script that you prepared. The script should just be a teaser: relatively short (typically not more than two pages in length) and with an engaging episode that will lure students to read the entire book.

Book talks should create excitement for books and alert students to the many possibilities found within the classroom or school library. For example, the following cliffhanger book talk by classroom teacher Janice Anderson really drums up interest in the three books presented:

Do you have someone in your life that makes you miserable? Well, you are not alone. Within these three books you will meet some characters who do some uncommon things to make others unhappy. In *The Araboolies of Liberty Street* (Swope, 2001), General Pinch and his wife are the nosey neighbors who insist on things going their way or else the General will "Call in the army!" In *Blue Cheese Breath and Stinky Feet: How to Deal With Bullies* (DePino, 2004), Steve is told that that is what he smells like. Lastly, in the *Recess Queen* (O'Neill, 2002), nobody swings, kicks, or bounces until Mean Jean says so.

Will there ever be freedom on Liberty Street? Does Steve really have blue cheese breath and stinky feet? Can the playground ever become a place to play?

Visit your bookstore or library today to get the answers for yourself... because nobody likes being miserable.

Interactive Read-Alouds. Interactive read-alouds are the second scheduled activity during community reading time. A number of studies demonstrate the motivational value of reading aloud to students (Artley, 1975; Gambrell, Codling, & Palmer, 1996; Ivey & Broaddus, 2001). Most of the time during these read-alouds, however, students simply listen to books rather than discuss them (Hoffman, Roser, & Battle, 1993). Interactive read-alouds, however, do more than motivate students. An interactive read-aloud engages students in actively thinking about texts rather than simply listening to them. Interactive read-alouds allow you to model for students the kinds of thinking they should be doing as they read on their own. Interactive read-alouds develop oral language (Pinnell & Jaggar, 2003) and contribute to student understanding of narrative discourse forms (Mandler, 1984; Nelson, 1986). Through the scaffolding provided by the read-aloud, students can often access the book independently.

The following guidelines can ensure successful interactive read-aloud experiences (Barrentine, 1996):

- Select books carefully. Interactive read aloud books should be selected on the basis of their quality, whether fiction or nonfiction. Books for younger readers might use rhythm, rhyme, and repetition. Fiction books should contain lively plots, engaging characters, and effective uses of language. Informational books should be connected to curricular topics in science, social studies, health, or mathematics. Informational books should be accurate in terms of both text and illustration and should not be dull; they should provide information in a way that captivates readers.

- Be familiar with the book. Before engaging students in an interactive read-aloud, familiarize yourself with the text, both its language and its vocabulary. Practice reading aloud if it does not come naturally to you. Also, you should carefully consider the literacy skills that can best be taught through the book. Reading aloud a book like *A Whale Is Not a Fish: And Other Animal Mix-Ups* (Berger, 1995), for example, provides a perfect opportunity to discuss the compare-and-contrast text structure using a text that contrasts a variety of often-confused animals. To promote understanding of contrast, you would point out the format of the text, which uses two-page, illustrated spreads to contrast the animals in question.

- Create before-reading activities. Before doing an interactive read-aloud, plan how you will prepare students for listening to the text. You can ask students to predict what the text will be about after reading the title, author's name, and book cover. You can have students do a picture walk-through of the text or, with informational texts, ask students to predict what the table of contents would include. You should introduce unfamiliar words and build background knowledge for the text using strategies such K-W-L (Ogle, 1986).

- Plan stopping points for questioning within the text. Before the interactive read-alouds, note the critical points where you need to explain, elaborate, and question students about the text, such as when students might need clarification for challenging concepts. Questioning students about the text provides the opportunity to assess student understanding, either to monitor student recall of factual information or to address more critical reading skills. For example, when reading the novel *Call It Courage* (Sperry, 1940) aloud to a group of fourth graders, you can ask students the following questions: Why do you think Mafatu decided to leave his village? Do you think this was a good decision? Why or why not? Later in the text, you can ask a factual recall question like, What were the challenges that Mafatu faced in this chapter?

- Plan ways to enrich or extend the text. After completing the interactive read-aloud, have multiple copies of the text available for students to read independently. In addition, you can find ways for students to build on what they have learned through other texts and media. Following the *Call It Courage* (Sperry, 1940) example, after the read-aloud, students might enjoy learning more about the Polynesian culture by exploring websites or creating their own storyboards using paper and markers. Students might then look online to examine the carved wooden storyboards found on many Polynesian islands. These storyboards are used to represent the events of the ancient traditional tales that continue to be told in many of the islands.

Time for Reading. Because the focus of community reading time is on developing motivation for reading rather than specific reading skill development, try to provide reading opportunities that focus on the pleasurable aspects of reading by giving students highly motivating materials like graphic novels and comic books.

Reading time might include practice in short choral reading of poems, reading short plays, performing Readers Theatre scripts based on books students would enjoy reading, oral reading of poems for two voices such as those by Paul Fleischman, or listening to online books for children. Reading online digital books like those found on the International Digital Children's Library website (en.childrenslibrary.org) can be very motivating for young readers, too. Students might also do paired reading of highly engaging titles like *The True Story of the 3 Little Pigs!* (Scieszka, 1989).

Book Sharing. Children need opportunities to share their reading experiences with others. These experiences can allow students to express their feelings about books as well as let their peers get ideas for books they can read. A simple way for students to share their reading is to allow three students daily to present their book to the group. Students can briefly summarize their book, describe their reaction to the book, and read a short, interesting excerpt to the class. Students might use a document camera to share favorite illustrations and retell the story, especially when reading picture books or graphic novels. Another way for students to share their reading is in small groups. Students could, for example, be grouped according to interests; students interested in books about sports could form a small book-sharing group. In this way students increase their familiarity with books they might wish to read in the future.

Another form of sharing might involve having students who have read the same book write and briefly perform a short Readers Theatre based on a small section of the book. All of these sharing activities have the effect of a pebble thrown into a pond: They widen the scope of children's reading, familiarizing them with the vast variety of potential reading choices available to them.

Informal Assessment and Record Keeping. Informal assessment of student progress during community reading time can help you stay informed about student progress. Assessments used during this time should focus largely on student motivation and the development of interest in reading. Maintaining anecdotal records as you observe students is all that is necessary; record keeping should be kept to a minimum to keep the focus of community reading time on maintaining motivation reading, rather than grading.

SIRT

SIRT involves four critical activities: focus lessons, time for reading, student–teacher reading conferences, and response to reading activities. A typical schedule for SIRT involves 15 minutes for a large-group focus lesson, 30 minutes for individual reading, and 15 minutes for student completion of response activities. Embedded within this time are individual student–teacher conferences, which can take about 15 minutes. Obviously this schedule may need to be modified depending upon the age of the students. Focus lessons delineate the strategies students practice during their reading, and students are given time to read and apply what they learn during these lessons. Because students work independently while you conference with other students, it is imperative that all students know what they are expected to accomplish during SIRT. Students need to be held accountable for their learning, so you should use conference time to carefully assess student growth in reading and writing, measure student progress, and ensure that students are using their time productively.

Focus Lesson Topics

Focus lessons are short lessons (15–20 minutes) related to procedures and literacy strategies. Regardless of the type of lesson, you need to model what students are to do, provide guided practice that supports students as they try out the strategy or procedure, and give opportunities for independent practice in performing the desired behavior. The following paragraphs describe topics for both procedural and strategy focus lessons, and Table 11 provides examples of possible focus lesson topics in each of these categories.

Procedural focus lessons acquaint students with procedures they need to know to get the maximum benefit from SIRT. These can include lessons on record keeping, conference preparation, how to work in centers during book response time, and a series of lessons on book selection. These

Table 11. Types of Focus Lessons

Procedural Lessons	Literacy Strategy Lessons
• Record keeping/maintaining the reading folder	• Figuring out new words
• Preparing for conferences	• Visualizing while reading
• Working in centers	• Retelling
• Using the computer center	• Reading fluently
• Selecting books	• Visualizing when you read
• Knowing when to abandon a book	• Understanding characters
• Finding your next book	• Making text-to-text connections
• Reading a range of genres	• Inferring from text
• Selecting informational books	• Skimming and scanning

lessons should be short, to the point, and model for students appropriate student behaviors.

Strategy focus lessons should be targeted at teaching and reinforcing strategic reading. Although Chapter 4 provides in-depth information on this topic, we provide a few topic ideas here, followed by two sample lessons. These focus lessons should provide a framework for student learning within the SIRT experience, and after each lesson students should practice the skills demonstrated during reading time. During these focus lessons you may be addressing strategies that are new to students or ones that students need more practice on, including those that students struggled with during shared or guided reading or ones that your formal and informal assessments have identified as clear areas of need for students.

A major theme for strategy focus lessons should be book selection. As discussed, it is essential that students know how to select appropriate books independently because independent reading is predicated on the idea of student choice, and because students are more motivated to read when they choose their own books (Guthrie & Wigfield, 2000). However, unguided choice can often lead to students selecting books well beyond their reading level (Donovan et al., 2000) or books of little interest to them. Poor student book choices can derail the most effective independent reading program because students get less actual time on task and fail to truly engage with texts. For this reason, we advocate a series of focus lessons related to particular aspects of book selection. The following segments give you ideas for modeling a range of strategies for book selection.

Skimming Through the Text. Focus lessons that teach students how to skim through a text can provide students with skills that can help them discover their interest in a book, determine the difficulty of the book, and understand how the text is organized. By modeling for students how to skim and scan the table of contents, the headings, and other features, students can make better decisions about the books that they select.

Focusing on Personal Interest. Students need to be able to evaluate books in terms of interest. Model for students how to peruse the title, the author, and the blurb on the back cover to get an idea about the topic of the book. You might also want to model looking through the text at the pictures as another way to explore the topic. Once students understand how to identify the general concept of the book, further explain how to evaluate the content to make sure it appeals to their interests.

Following this focus lesson, have your students maintain a list of reading interests and potential titles of interest in their reading folder. This list can be added to after book talks, after conferences (which are a good time to recommend books to your students based on their interest survey from Chapter 2), after student book sharing, or after interactive read-alouds.

Evaluating for Difficulty. It is essential that students select books of appropriate difficulty, so a focus lesson that teaches them how to do so is important. Teach students the Goldilocks rule (Taberski, 2000; see Chapter 2), for example, along with the concept that there are three different types of texts: easy, just right, and challenging. The five-finger test can be used along with the Goldilocks rule to provide students with another measure of the difficulty of a book they may be considering. (See Chapter 2 for more discussion of both the Goldilocks rule and the five-finger test.) Figure 2 is a checklist made by one fourth-grade class to help determine if a text was just right.

Figure 2. Checklist for Just Right Books

☐ The book is on a topic that interests me.

☐ The genre of the book is one that I like.

☐ I am familiar with the author, the characters, or the topic of the book.

☐ I know most of the words.

☐ I can figure out the words I do not know.

☐ My teacher or a friend told me about the book.

☐ The pictures or visuals help me understand the text.

☐ I understand the story or information in the book.

☐ I can read at a normal pace.

Selecting Peer-Recommended Texts. Although we believe in the importance of having students recommend books to one another, it is not always appropriate for students to read a peer recommended text. By modeling for students how to evaluate peer-recommended texts for level of difficulty, for interest, and for comprehension, students develop the ability to discriminate between those peer-recommended books that work for them and those that do not.

Using Online Resources to Select Books. You might choose to provide a focus lesson that addresses ways that students can select books using online resources. You can bookmark specific sites and then model for students how to use those sites. Students can read children's reviews of books online on The Spaghetti Book Club (spaghettibookclub.org), they can view the interiors of books at Amazon.com, or they can find teacher- and parent-recommended books at sites such as Reading Rockets (www .readingrockets.org/books) or Kids Reads (www.kidsreads.com).

Sample Focus Lessons

Identifying Character Traits. Third-grade teacher Maria Ruiz's students had been involved in independent reading since the beginning of the school year. Her students, many of whom were ELLs, had just begun to read longer chapter books that contained more developed characters than in the shorter books they had been reading up to this point. Maria decided to teach a focus lesson on character traits designed to help her students recognize that many characters in literature are multidimensional rather than one dimensional.

Maria began the lesson by reviewing with her students what a character is and some of the ways that readers learn about characters, such as through their appearance, what they say, and what they do. She recorded the name Opal on chart paper and listed the three headings Appearance, What They Say, and What They Do on the chart paper. Using the book *Because of Winn Dixie* (DiCamillo, 2001), she modeled for her students how to analyze Opal's character by reading aloud the first chapter of this book. She began by asking students to pay attention to the author's description of Opal, what she said, and what she did. Then the class filled in the chart as a group.

Using Headings to Read Informational Texts. Third-grade teacher Karyn Martin had been using an independent reading program for about three months. She conducted focus lessons for her students and conferenced with them regularly. Up until this point, most of her students selected fictional stories during SIRT. She had just completed a unit on informational texts, and she noted that more and more students were opting to read these texts. Although Karyn had presented guided reading lessons on reading informational texts, she noticed that those students who did select informational texts had difficulty staying focused on the content. For this reason, she decided to teach a focus lesson on how to read to answer questions based on text headings.

Karyn began her lesson by explaining to students that during this week they were to select an informational trade book for independent reading time. She had a large collection of such books in the classroom library, and she made a point of conducting book talks on these books during community reading time.

During the focus lesson she pointed to the location of the informational books in the classroom library and explained that informational books are about real-world topics such as fish, birds, machines, hobbies, history, and more. Then she opened discussion of the main features of informational text: challenging words, specific organizational structure, tables of contents, headings, and photos or graphics. She explained some of the features of informational text that help the reader, like headings being boldfaced or large-print words telling important ideas. Karyn then modeled reading the book *Poison Dart Frogs* (Reeder, 2005). She pointed out that the table of contents reveals that this book contains a chapter on the life cycle of poison dart frogs, a flow diagram, and also a news report on poison dart frogs. She modeled how to find a chapter using the table of contents and turning to the indicated page, and then she demonstrated a few of the headings and subheadings throughout the chapter. She wrote the headings as questions on sticky notes, explaining that this was a good way to find information and remember it.

As Karyn read the section aloud, she noted that amphibians are cold blooded, take in oxygen through their skin, and spend time on land and in the water. She recorded these as bulleted notes on the board. She then turned the page and noted the subheading. She again modeled how to turn this heading into a question and then read to find the answer. She thought aloud about what she learned about the birth of the frog throughout this section. She continued reading and taking notes on the rest of the chapter in this way.

After she had followed this process, Karyn invited students to work with a partner to create questions from headings in the section of the text labeled Poison Dart Frog Behaviors. Following this, she guided students in selecting their own informational trade book at an appropriate level for independent reading. She gave students a large sticky note and asked them to create questions from the headings in one part of their book. Students were instructed to read to find the answer to the question in the heading and jot it down on the sticky note. She instructed students to create these heading questions in their minds and then read to find the answer. She reminded students that she would check their understanding of this strategy during their individual conference time.

Time for Reading

During time for reading, students do two things: (1) They practice reading in an appropriate book while applying what they learned during the focus lessons, and (2) they participate with you in a conference. Students can read at their desks, or you can provide students with comfortable areas for reading.

Students should have their books selected and ready to read at the beginning of this 30-minute block of time. If at all possible, students should read silently. With younger students, you might want to break up reading time into two parts: 15 minutes for silent or whisper reading and 15 minutes for paired reading.

During reading time, students may have the option to read any book, or their choices can be limited to books that fit the lesson plan. For example, if you want students to work on their ability to analyze characters, direct students to select fiction books with strong, well-developed characters. Make sure to prepare this selection ahead of time and place the titles on a special bookshelf in the classroom library so they are easy for students to identify.

Student–Teacher Conferences

Teacher-led conferences are the centerpiece of the independent reading program. Reading conferences provide a connection to the larger reading program and promote the goal of creating lifelong readers. Reading conferences are typically short blocks of time (5–15 minutes) that occur in the 30 minutes of student reading, during which teachers meet individually with students. There might be additional times throughout the day when you can conduct reading conferences, such as guided reading group time or center time.

Teacher conferences provide both time to monitor student progress toward a variety of literacy goals, general and specific, as well as the opportunity to work individually with students—ongoing support is necessary to move them toward true independence as readers. During these conferences, you can effectively assess students' progress in terms of motivation, attitude toward reading, ability to select and engage with texts, use of reading strategies, oral fluency, and narrative and expository text comprehension. By considering each student's progress in this holistic way, you are able to evaluate the student in terms of the entirety of his or her reading performance rather than focusing on a single literacy skill. During this time, you may find it useful to question students, conduct running records, review student written responses to texts, and so on. Conferences should be based on what you know about the student and his or her reading abilities so you can address areas of strength and need.

Reading conferences can be held at a designated place in the classroom library, or at a student's desk, or a favorite reading spot. Holding conferences at your own desk can be intimidating, especially for younger readers.

Conferences allow for differentiated instruction suited to the needs of the student, which allows conferences to focus on many different areas. For example, a conference may focus on assessing a broad literacy goal such as student motivation for reading, or it might focus on evaluating narrower skills like ways to decode unfamiliar words. Some areas might be easily addressed in one or two conferences, although others, such as oral fluency, might require attention over a period of months.

The following sections provide ideas about what to do during conferences. The first conference idea is based on book selection, which is connected to the procedural focus lesson(s) on book selection described earlier. The second conference idea addresses students' reading and fluency in the context of the specific book they are reading. In addition to these two types of conference ideas, there are many other types of conferences you can use with individual students, such as focusing on a particular comprehension skill like visualization, a decoding skill like figuring out new words, or a comparison of two different books that a student has read. Students themselves might request conferences on different topics. For example, a student who needs help getting out of a reading rut might request a conference so that you can recommend books from different genres that might be of interest. The focus of conferences should be determined by both you and the student, based on student needs.

Book-Selection Conference. Either at the beginning of the school year or during the implementation of an independent reading program, you should provide students with focus lessons on book selection and appropriate behavior during independent reading time. As a follow up to these focus lessons, you might wish to make selecting appropriate reading materials the target strategy for a reading conference. Such a conference might be appropriate for "in a rut" readers who read the same genre over and over, for students who have difficulty selecting books, or for those students who are not reading during independent reading time. The purpose of this conference could include any or all of the following:

- To gather additional data about the ways in which a particular student selects a book
- To assess a student's ability to effectively select a text
- To explore difficulties a student encounters in using independent reading time effectively

You can prepare for this meeting by following these suggestions:

- Review the student's Reading Log (see Appendix A) and genre wheel (see Chapter 2).
- Review the student's Reading Interest Form (see Appendix A).
- Review any anecdotal notes recorded during community reading time or other times during the day.

There are many ways to engage students during a conference to assess their understand of focus lessons, maintain their motivation, and evaluate their ability to apply what they have learned. During this conference you could do the following:

- Ask the student to read aloud for one minute while you take a running record.
- Review with the student the Reading Interest Form. Have the student identify his or her reading interests and discuss the level of interest in the book he or she has been reading.
- Ask the student to explain the processes used for selecting recent reading materials, or give the student several books and ask for an explanation of how to go about selecting an appropriate book.
- Review with the student some of the strategies that have been addressed during the focus lessons.
- Guide the student in selecting a new book.
- Record anecdotal notes on the Reading Conference Record (see Appendix A).

Book-Focused Conference. Most conferences focus on assessing student success in reading their independent reading books. At these conferences, focus on helping students set reading goals, evaluating student's fluency, and assessing student's understanding. In the example that follows, the teacher conducts a book conference with a gifted fourth-grade reader. She begins the conference with completion of a running record to assess fluency, and then asks the student a series of questions designed to evaluate his understanding of the book. Questions were selected from the list provided in Table 12.

Table 12. Reading Conference Comprehension Questions

Response Questions	Literary Elements Questions
• Why did you pick this book? • Did the book meet your expectations? Why or why not? • Would you tell a friend to read this book? Why or why not? • What would you tell a friend about the book?	• Who were the main characters in the book? • Did they change during the story? How? • Where and when did the story take place? • What problems did the main character face? Did you like the way the character solved those problems? Why or why not? • What was your favorite part of the book? • Did you like the ending? Why or why not?

"Miguel, please show me your reading folder and the book you have been reading. I see that you completed three books during the past three weeks, and they all were chapter books. You indicated here that you enjoyed all of these books because they were about boys your own age and they were fantasies. I know how much you liked the Harry Potter books, so I'm very interested in learning about your response to *The Lightning Thief: Percy Jackson and the Olympians* (Riordan, 2005). Show me the book you have been reading for this week. How many pages have you read so far?" she asks.

Miguel hands the teacher the book. "I have read 50 pages so far," he says.

"Good job, Miguel. Your goal for this week was 40 pages, so you have done well. Today I'm going to ask you to read aloud to me for one minute from your book. I am going to take notes while you read." At this point, the teacher completes the running record while the student reads and then shares her results with the student. "Miguel, you missed only two words, so that tells me that this book is at the right level for you." She shares the words Miguel missed to see if he might be able to identify his errors.

"Now I would like to ask you some questions about the book you were reading. Could you tell me why you chose this book?"

"Well, I chose it because I had read all the Harry Potter books, and you told me that this book was a fantasy like Harry Potter, only about gods and goddesses. It sounded good."

"Where did the story take place?"

"Well, it took place in New York, but they went to lots of different places when they were on the quest, like Denver, Las Vegas, and Los Angeles."

"Who were the main characters?"

"They were Percy Jackson, who is the son of Poseidon and a human mom. The other characters were Annabeth and Grover. They went with Percy on his quest."

"Did you think that Percy changed as the story went on?"

"Yes, I think he got braver, less clumsy, and more grown up. He seemed to keep his cool more at the end of the book than at the beginning."

"What was your favorite part of the book?"

"My favorite part was when Percy met his father, Poseidon. During the meeting you felt like Percy's father did care about him, even though Percy wasn't sure about that."

"Did you like the way Percy solved the problems he had?"

"Yes, he used his brain a lot. He was very smart and good at figuring things out. But he also had help from his magic sword and from his friends. "

"Did you like the ending? Why or why not?" the teacher asked.

"I liked it because it told who the real lightning thief was. I think it sort of hinted that there would be more trouble with Kronos, too."

At this point the teacher asks Miguel to set his reading goal for the following week, and she praises his excellent comprehension of the book. She also suggests that he complete a book response activity with another student who has read *The Lightning Thief* (Riordan, 2005).

Response to Reading Activities

Students need to share what they have read with their peers in order to create a community of readers, or to interact with a larger community of readers. These book-sharing experiences can take many different forms, such as the completion of graphic organizers appropriate to a particular text (see Chapter 4) or other artistic responses to texts. Students might also employ technology in creating responses, using PowerPoint to create presentations about their books. They might maintain a blog as they read, or they might respond to the text by e-mailing a friend who is reading the same book. Many websites post children's book reviews, and author websites allow students to gain information about the authors of the books they read. Older students might become involved in fanfiction.net and create their own stories based on the book they read.

Assessment and Record Keeping

During SIRT, students are responsible for maintaining records that they keep in their reading folders and bring to their reading conferences, such as the following:

- Reading Interest Forms
- Reading Logs
- Response to reading materials
- Self-evaluation rubrics

As mentioned earlier, students record reading topics of interest and book titles that they would like to read on the Reading Interest Forms. Students keep records of all reading they do during the year, whether during SIRT or other times. In their Reading Logs, students maintain records of the books they have read as well as their evaluations of those books. In addition, students keep copies of their responses to reading (e.g., graphic organizers they have completed, book reviews they have written) in their folders. Finally, students should self-evaluate their weekly performance on the Independent Reading Self-Evaluation Rubric. This form lets students assess their performance in many different areas, including book selection, goal setting, and comprehension. It also contains room for student comments. Because your own record keeping is essential to documenting your students' progress during independent reading, we recommend completing the Independent Reading Observation Rubric for Teachers for each student each week. (All of the record-keeping forms mentioned here appear as reproducibles in Appendix A.)

By comparing the self-evaluation rubrics and teacher rubrics, both you and your students can see whether students are making progress in each area. Furthermore, you can compare your scores with your students and discuss areas of discrepancy and ways to improve students' independent reading.

In addition, you need to record notes from each conference on the Reading Conference Record form (see Appendix A for a reproducible), which provides space for completing running records as well as student responses to comprehension questions. Like the evaluation rubrics, comparison of these forms over time can demonstrate student growth in terms of both fluency and comprehension.

Good teachers create effective independent reading programs by motivating student reading, guiding student book choices, conducting effective conferences, maintaining careful records, and encouraging response to literature. Careful organization of an independent reading program ensures that students get to read self-selected materials but remain accountable for that reading. A well-organized and implemented independent reading program lets students practice reading and develop a love of reading while they improve their reading skills and abilities.

A DISCUSSION WITH LINDA B. GAMBRELL

Linda B. Gambrell is a professor at Clemson University. Her research interests are in the areas of literacy motivation, reading comprehension strategy instruction, and the role of discussion in teaching and learning; she has published numerous books, book chapters, and articles on these topics, and her research on motivation is quite relevant to this book. Gambrell is the only person elected to serve as president of the three leading literacy organizations in the United States: College Reading Association (1981–1982), National Reading Conference (1999–2000), and the International Reading Association (2007–2008).

Terrell Young: What is the best advice that you have for teachers regarding how they can maximize the effectiveness of independent reading?

Linda Gambrell: First, I suspect that one of the reasons past research has not yielded highly positive results for independent reading is that just giving students time to read is not enough. In order for independent reading to support reading development, the teacher must be actively working with students—helping them learn how to select appropriate books, having conferences, listening to children read from books they have selected, and sharing good books that will interest and challenge students. This is particularly true during the primary grades when some children have not yet learned how to make good decisions about what they can read successfully. During those developmental years, the teacher has to take a more active role in helping children learn to make good choices about what they read.

Second, individual conferences are critical to the success of independent reading time. Scheduling conferences with students takes time, but it shows that the teacher is interested in what students are reading and appreciates that they are making appropriate text selections.

TY: How important is student book choice?

LG: The more you read the better reader you become. If a student always chooses books that are too difficult or far too easy, he or she will not get the practice that is needed to become a fluent reader. In schools where I have worked where independent reading time is an important part of the reading curriculum, the teachers work very hard to help support students in learning how to make good book choices. Students are also responsible for keeping track of the books they read during independent reading time. The students don't have to write a book report. Instead, they write a brief comment about the book, and they indicate whether the book was just right, too easy, or challenging.

It is important to sensitize children to the fact that we all read books across all those levels. If I am particularly interested in spiders, then I might want or need to read a book that is a bit difficult, but because I'm really, really interested in spiders I can tackle it and get some information out of it. It is also fine to read books that are easy some of the time. But most of the independent reading time should be spent with books and materials that are just right. Independent reading time can provide the practice that will help students learn how to choose books that are appropriate. One of my concerns with the leveled reading materials and programs is that students may be missing out on opportunities to learn how to select appropriate books. In the real world, there is not always going to be someone around to give them books on their reading level.

TY: Based on your own research, what message would you give to teachers regarding the use of awards and incentives for reading?

LG: My words of advice would be that we must be careful about what we use as incentives or rewards. Research by Fawson and Moore (1999) about a decade ago, reports that nearly 95% of teachers used some kind of reward or incentive program to motivate children to read. I really think some of those incentives are fine. I'm sure if I were teaching young children today, I would be the first one to sign up for the pizza program. Everybody loves a little pizza or a few M&Ms. What we have to understand is that the rewards we use reflect our values. Things of "high value" are used as rewards. Kids love pizza. The pizza people know what they are doing! If a student reads a number of books, they get a free pizza. The message this sends is that pizza is really important—it is highly valued.

Our goal should be to support and help children see the value of reading and literacy. That means we need to find ways to make reading a reward. I see teachers who are doing a wonderful job of that. In their class, they will have good guided reading time where everyone is very productive so the teacher will say, "You did such a great job during guided reading today! All of our groups have worked hard and were very productive. I'm going to give you a reward by reading an extra chapter in *The Bridge to Terabithia* [Paterson, 1977] aloud." What that teacher has done is make *reading* the reward. There are others ways to make reading the reward, such as giving students an additional five minutes of independent reading time. If we want children to value reading, then *reading* needs to be the incentive or the reward.

TY: After the National Reading Panel report, many people have suggested that independent reading should take place outside of school so the literacy block can focus on instruction. What is your response to that suggestion?

LG: I believe the NRP has been misinterpreted to some extent. They acknowledge the limitations of their survey of the research. The report does acknowledge that there are literally hundreds of studies that show a correlation between time spent reading and reading achievement. The NRP did not include correlational or descriptive studies, for example, which limited their findings to the five focus areas: phonemic awareness, phonics, vocabulary, fluency, and comprehension. Unfortunately, some people interpreted the report in a way that I think was off target. They took that report and said, "There are few random-trial experimental studies to show that independent reading time in schools pays off, so we probably do not need to spend time on it." That is a misinterpretation of the NPR. There is, in fact, a large body of research to support time spent reading in school.

I think the one thing that we all know is that the amount of time that children have spent with someone reading to them and talking with them about what they have just read, correlates very, very highly with their success in school, and especially literacy development. Once children are in school, how do we make up that gap between the "lucky" students who have had those experiences, and the "unlucky" students who haven't been raised in an environment where there was an adult who has nurtured their literacy development? Including teacher read-aloud time and independent reading time during the school day is critical for many students, especially for struggling readers and ELLs. Not to do so disenfranchises the struggling literacy learner.

I am a big fan of Malcolm Gladwell. When I was reading his recent book *Outliers: The Story of Success* (Gladwell, 2008), all I could think about was how much the ideas in the book apply to children's literacy development. His major thesis is that you have to really practice something over and over and over again to become skilled. He writes about people who spend more than 10,000 hours practicing something to become good at their craft—whether it is Tiger Woods in golf, Bill Gates and computer technology, or The Beatles and music. The same principle applies to children and their reading development. You need lots of practice reading to get good at reading. What better way to promote that practice than by providing students with a well-organized independent reading time.

I also must say that just giving students 15–20 minutes a day to read books of their choice is probably not going to pay off in terms of increasing reading achievement. But there are dividends when the teacher supports, scaffolds, and inspires students to read. There is a whole litany of things that needs to be embedded in independent reading time to make it effective—choice, time to talk about what has been read, learning to choose appropriate books, and so on.

I'm a firm believer that every good reading program includes teacher read-alouds, teacher guided instruction, scaffolded reading instruction, and independent reading time that allows students to practice reading. Whatever we do for reading instruction has to be solid, systematic, and balanced. I think independent reading is a key component of students' daily reading instruction. We actually call it monitored self-selected reading, emphasizing the important role that the teacher plays in guiding, nurturing, and supporting children during their independent reading. It is not just free reading time; it is teacher-supported reading time.

TY: Why are classroom libraries so important to independent reading?

LG: Oh, I think the role of the classroom library cannot be over estimated. But a high-quality classroom library is more than just having lots of good books. I love it when teachers have funds to increase the number of books in their classroom libraries. I think that is a very good use of funds. Having lots of good books is vital to a successful classroom library. Let me add that I think it is very important that the books be current, and reflect what's hot. As adults, we love to read the new bestsellers. My point here is that children are aware of new books and books that are up to date. I think we have to treat our classroom libraries like we treat our clothes closets. Many of us buy lots of clothes and lots of shoes, but when we walk into our closets we say, "Oh! I don't have anything to wear!" One of the reasons is we haven't cleaned out our clothes closet. We can't see the good stuff because we have everything crammed in the closet. I think we need to work more on culling our classroom libraries. I have been in classrooms where I know there are hundreds of books that children's hands have never touched. They're old and they're out of date. Of course, there are some classics that we always want to keep but we need to cull our classroom libraries so that children can see and find the really good books.

What I really love to see is teachers doing something special with old books. For example, teachers can take some of the books that are dated and put hot pink tape on the spine. On special occasions, such as St. Valentine's Day or the first day of winter, the teacher might say, "Because you have been doing so well during independent reading time I'm going to give each of you a reward. Everyone gets to pick out one of the hot pink books to take home for your very own." We can get rid of those old books and make them special by giving them to the children. This accomplishes two things. First, this gives students a special book that they can read at home over a holiday. Second, the teacher is giving a "reward" that communicates that reading and books are valued. I worked with a teacher who bought 150 new books for the classroom library every year. She then selected 150 "old" books from her classroom library and let every child choose a special book at Thanksgiving, Christmas, spring break, and on his or her birthday. In doing so, she kept her classroom collection current and helped each of the students to develop a home library.

TY: Would you please comment on your study in which you asked students about where they typically found their favorite books?

LG: I published a study in 1995 on children's reading habits where we asked students in grades 1, 3, 5, and 8 about favorite books they had read recently. It couldn't be a book their teacher read aloud or one that their parents read to them—it had to be a book that they read themselves. As a part of our study, we recorded the titles of the books, and we then asked them, "Where did you get that book?" I don't remember the exact percentage, but it was well over 90% of the children who reported that they got the book from their classroom library. We know that school, home, and community libraries are all important, but in our study, we found that the books children became deeply involved in reading came primarily from classroom libraries. I think this speaks to how important the classroom library really is in a child's literacy development. If you think about it, the classroom is where children spend most of their time, so that's where they are going to have a few minutes here and there to find books to read and enjoy.

CHAPTER 4

Linking Strategic Literacy Instruction With Independent Reading

This chapter explores ways that you can use the gradual release of responsibility (GRR) model (Pearson & Gallagher, 1983) to link literacy instruction with independent reading experiences. It describes how strategies taught during modeled reading, guided reading, and shared reading experiences can be transferred to the independent reading experiences. Researchers frequently note that the most effective teachers provide scaffolded instruction, during which they "give high support for students practicing new [strategies] and then slowly decreasing that support to increase student ownership and self-sufficiency" (Biancarosa & Snow, 2004, p. 14). Such teachers hold student independence as their goal and the measure of success. The GRR model is often used to give students the support needed to become independent. This chapter also incorporates response to reading activities including journal writing, using mentor texts for writing, creative dramatics, response activities that incorporate technology (e.g., creating wikis), and incorporating the arts into responses.

The GRR Model

Engaged readers need instruction that helps them develop literacy and enables them to think deeply about their reading and writing (Young, 2006b). One fifth-grade student in Bellevue, Washington noted, "I used to read like a water skier skimming across the surface. Now, I read like a scuba diver." His teacher, a member of a professional learning community studying *Mosaic of Thought: The Power of Comprehension Strategy Instruction* (Keene & Zimmermann, 2007), had taught him strategies in a profoundly different way that enable him to plumb the depths of the text.

Typically, exemplary teachers focus on fewer strategies and teach them thoroughly (Keene, 2008). For instance, comprehension strategies generally include the following: building background knowledge/ making connections, constructing mental images, inferring, determining importance, predicting, summarizing and synthesizing, monitoring, and evaluating (Allington, 2006; Harvey & Goudvis, 2007; Keene & Zimmermann, 2007; Oczkus, 2004). You are most effective when your instruction includes "teacher explanations and modeling of strategies, with scaffolded student practice in strategies application of a long period of time" (Pressley, 2002, p. 280). Often the guided practice or scaffolding takes place in small groups or with partners involving "student conversations, rich in student reports of how they are applying strategies and their internalization of the strategic processes" (Pressley, 2002, p. 280). Table 13 demonstrates the GRR model.

Reading Aloud

When you read aloud in your classroom, you allow your students to experience books they could not read on their own (Mooney, 1990). Reading aloud models reading for students so that students have opportunities to see proficient readers' strategies.

Mooney (2004) points out that books chosen for this "approach usually [have] more challenges for students than elements that would support their reading" (p. 78). Some books lure students to revisit them again and again, so take great care in selecting books to read aloud (Young, 2006a). "Reading to students is comparable to the optimum advertisement for books as incomparable presents," notes Mooney (2004, p. 78). You need to carefully consider your purpose for reading aloud, your curriculum, and your students' interests and prior literature experiences when selecting books for this approach.

Shared Reading

In shared reading, students receive the support necessary to be successful in activities they could not do independently. Appropriate for both whole- and small-group experiences, shared reading allows students to unpack the processes and prepares them to take more responsibility with your support. Miller (2006) notes that students sometimes learn about a strategy, skill, or procedure through a teacher demonstration, but they do not have the depth of understanding to actually apply what

Table 13. GRR Model for Strategy Instruction

Teacher-Regulated	⟺		Student-Regulated
Approaches			
Reading aloud	Shared reading	Guided reading	Independent reading
The teacher reads aloud, stopping periodically to model the strategy through a think-aloud.	The teacher and students practice the strategy together with the teacher reading and students helping to think through the text.	The teacher provides support as the students read in small groups.	Students apply their knowledge and strategies while reading alone or with partners.
• The teacher gives an explanation of the strategy. • The teacher demonstrates with a brief modeling of how the strategy is used to understand text.	• The teacher purposely guides large-group discussion. • The teacher scaffolds the students' attempts to use the strategy and provides support and feedback.	• The teacher guides students' use of the strategy providing support as needed. • Students share how the strategy helped them while reading. • The teacher assesses and responds to students' needs.	• Students use strategies on their own and with partners. • Students and the teacher provide feedback. • Students apply strategy across genres, settings, and contests.
I do, you watch.	I do, you help.	You do, I help.	You do, I watch.
Text selection			
Teacher choice	Teacher choice	Managed choice (but carefully matched to students' needs)	Student choice

Note. Adapted from Harvey & Goudvis, 2007; Mooney, 1990, 2004; Pearson & Gallagher, 1983; Wilhelm, Baker, & Dube, 2001

they have learned to their own reading. Shared reading provides some students with the opportunity to learn the skills at such depth they can use them in their own work. For others, additional scaffolding is necessary through guided reading.

Guided Reading

Guided reading enables students to try certain skills and strategies with your support. Allington (2009a) states, "Here the teacher typically selects the texts to be read, offers guidance before the students read, monitors student performance while reading, and follows up after reading with additional guidance or assessment activities" (p. 42). Thompson (2005) has suggestions for making considerations when planning, conducting, and evaluating a guided reading session. Before meeting with the students, you should do the following:

- Determine the purpose and strategy based on an analysis of students' strengths and needs and your anecdotal notes from observations and previous guided reading sessions.
- Choose a text that is appropriate for the students' strengths and needs, your purpose, and the selected strategy.
- Plan how you will introduce the text and your purpose as well as the reading and discussion.

During the session with the student, you should do the following:

- Introduce the text selection, share the goal of the lesson, and set the purpose for reading.
- Monitor and observe the students' reading.
- Involve the students in discussing the selection and sharing their response to the text and the selected strategy.
- Review what the students have learned.

After the session with the student, you should do the following:

- Reflect on how the session met its goals and purpose.
- Evaluate the students' engagement and strategy use.
- Record notes on students' progress and identified needs.
- Organize follow-up activities if needed.
- Plan further teaching activities for future guided reading lessons.

We offer here a note of caution: During guided reading instruction do not keep students dependent upon you and your support to complete the task at hand. Only provide support when needed rather than control the students' reading.

Independent Reading

For far too many students, limited reading takes place outside the classroom. For them, instructional activities represent the only opportunities to read and write (RAND Reading Study Group, 2002). Indeed, Hiebert and Martin (2009) note that students may spend as little as 7–18 minutes per day reading, even in schools that dedicate 90 minutes to literacy instruction. As they point out, "In fact, the mandates for longer reading periods could even, unintentionally, result in lower reading levels if students become increasingly disengaged by spending long periods of time in tedious or trivial practice tasks" (p. 5).

Moreover, independent reading provides students with the opportunities to practice the full act of reading (Cunningham & Allington, 2007). While instruction may focus on inferring word meaning or synthesizing information, independent reading provides students with the opportunity to apply the skills and strategies that they have learned through teacher modeling as well as shared and guided reading. This time is critically important for students' success as readers. Guthrie (2004) notes that it is often the amount of practice that distinguishes an expert reader from a novice.

At the end of independent reading time, many teachers have a sharing time where students share how they applied strategies. Keene (2008) states that it is not enough for students to share which strategy they attempted during their independent reading time. Instead, they need to do the following:

- Describe how using that particular strategy helped strengthen their comprehension and how that strategy could be useful for future readings.
- Identify what that strategy helped them to comprehend in the piece.
- Note the conditions that contributed to their comprehension (e.g., small-group discussions or silent contemplation) and how re-creating those conditions could help future comprehension.

The GRR Model in Action: Looking in One Classroom

Nicole Blake now teaches third grade students in Richland, Washington. Her previous teaching experiences included teaching students in fourth grade and a multiage classroom. She notes that her strategy instruction changes from year to year on the basis of both her increased understanding of strategy instruction and the needs of her students. The following section provides a glimpse into how Mrs. Blake teaches her students to infer.

When teaching students who do not have strong reading skills, Mrs. Blake often begins by sharing pictures with her students and asking the students to predict the feelings and emotions of those in the photographs. They discuss the facial clues that helped them determine the subjects' feelings. She always emphasizes that her students need evidence to support their inferences. Later, students draw pictures where their peers can make inferences. For instance, one student drew a picture of herself flying a kite on a beach. The students inferred that it was warm because the girl was wearing shorts, that it was sunny because there was a shadow, that there was probably some wind because the kite was in the sky, and that she was happy because she was smiling.

Later, the students play charades where they use facial expressions to provide clues to the emotion they are attempting to portray. Sometimes this is followed by speaking lines to illustrate fear, impatience, anger, or other feelings. At other times, Mrs. Blake puts a word (e.g., *happy, sad, afraid*) on a student's back and that student asks his or her classmates questions to help determine the feeling. The classmates respond only with "yes" or "no." Sample questions include, "Would I feel this way if someone gave me something I really like?" "Would I feel this way if my football team won a game against a team with a better record?" The student then tries to guess the word posted on his or her back. The students practiced inferring through viewing, representing, listening, and speaking before they began using the strategy in reading.

Modeling With Poetry

Mrs. Blake typically models inference first using poetry. She often chooses poems about birds, insects, or animals and removes all references to the subject of the poem. She models how to use a schema to infer the poem's subject while displaying the poem without the title, illustrations, and references to the subject. Then she reads aloud portions of the poem, stopping frequently to share her thinking and evidence to support it. She models one and then does some together as a class. Later, she copies poems for the students and asks them to circle clues in the text to make an inference. She often uses the following poetry collections as sources for her poems for modeling inferring: Heard's (1992) *Creatures of Earth, Sea, and Sky: Animal Poems*; Dotlich's (2001) *When Riddles Come Rumbling: Poems to Ponder*; and Prelutsky's (2004) *If Not for the Cat*.

Modeling With Picture Books

After her students experience success inferring with poetry, Mrs. Blake is ready to model using picture books. Some of her favorites include Bunting's (1989) *The Wednesday Surprise,* Fox's (1996) *Feathers and Fools,* and Repchuk's (1997) *The Forgotten Garden.*

Mrs. Blake uses anchor charts—large visuals that teachers and students construct together—to make students' thinking permanent and visible. She uses the charts when modeling a new strategy and then involves her students in adding their comments to it. Anchor charts also serve as resources for students' ongoing use throughout a unit of study. Although anchor charts look similar to graphic organizers, they differ in that an anchor chart is used during instruction, posted in the classroom for all to see and use, and is coconstructed by the entire class. Graphic organizers, on the other hand, are used by individuals, partners, and small groups when practicing or applying a skill or strategy. Both anchor charts and graphic organizers are important tools for strategy instruction and learning. Figure 3 shows an anchor chart for the book *Feathers and Fools.*

Mrs. Blake's students continue to add to the anchor chart with each day's new thinking noted in another color. She sometimes writes what her students are sharing on sticky notes rather than directly on the chart for management purposes; by using the sticky notes, she does not have to turn her back to the students while writing their comments. The many anchor charts posted in the room allow her students to keep a record of their thinking (some of these ideas are adapted from those found in *Reading With Meaning: Teaching Comprehension in the Primary Grades* [Miller, 2002]).

She tells her students to watch and listen carefully as she models inferring in the book *The Forgotten Garden* (Repchuk, 1997). Her students

Figure 3. Anchor Chart for *Feathers and Fools*

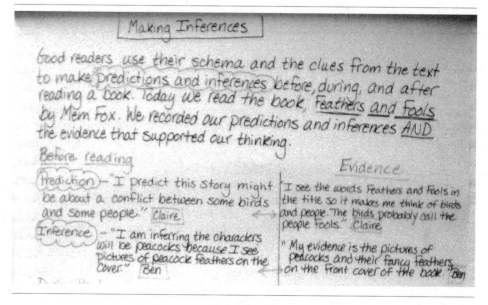

Making Inferences

Good readers use their schema and the clues from the text to make predictions and inferences before, during, and after reading a book. Today we read the book, Feathers and Fools by Mem Fox. We recorded our predictions and inferences AND the evidence that supported our thinking.

Before reading

Evidence

Prediction – "I predict this story might be about a conflict between some birds and some people." Claire

"I see the words Feathers and Fools in the title so it makes me think of birds and people. The birds probably call the people fools." Claire

Inference – "I am inferring the characters will be peacocks because I see pictures of peacock feathers on the cover." Ben

" My evidence is the pictures of peacocks and their fancy feathers on the front cover of the book." Ben

know that they will later discuss what they observed and how the strategy will help them as readers (Harvey & Goudvis, 2007). She reads a few pages into the text and stops to model her thinking. Table 14 provides a sampling of text and Mrs. Blake's thinking aloud to model the strategy. She reminds her students that inferences are supported with both a schema and evidence from the text. She notes that this creates a deeper conversation from what students have experienced in the earlier grades. She reminds them of how this conversation should look different from a conversation they had the previous year.

Shared Reading

Mrs. Blake models her thinking a few times and completes reading only part of the text. Often her students are eager to try their hands at the strategy, so she switches to shared reading and continues to read on, stopping at appropriate places to invite students to share their thinking by asking, "What inferences can you make?"

Sometimes she reads a harder book and lets the students think aloud when she stops reading. In doing so, the students share how their

Table 14. Example of Mrs. Blake's Think-Aloud for *The Forgotten Garden*

Text Example—*The Forgotten Garden* (Repchuk, 1997, u.p.)	Mrs. Blake's Think-Aloud
"He stood, frozen in time, and recalled a garden so beautiful it had charmed the birds from the skies and the beasts from the fields beyond. Now beauty stood strangled by neglect. Gone were the rustlings of life, the blaze of color and the birdsong."	I am inferring that these words "He stood, frozen in time, and recalled a garden so beautiful," mean this man has not been to this garden in a long time. I know the word "recalled" means to remember and the words "frozen in time" make me think he is remembering a time he spent in the garden years ago. I am predicting that this garden might be from his childhood. I can infer that this garden used to be extra special if it "charmed the birds from the skies and the beasts from the fields beyond." The picture on this page shows the garden in black and white. It is hard to tell, but I am inferring by the picture that the man is recalling some of the beautiful images from how the garden used to be. You have to look closely at the picture to see the blurred sketches in the background. The words "now beauty stood strangled by neglect" make me think it has been years and years since anyone has cared for the garden. I know the word "neglect" means to not care for something properly. The word "strangled" can mean to stifle or stop the development of something. It can also mean to cut off the oxygen of something living. I am inferring that the author carefully chose the words "strangled by neglect" to make a point that this garden was dead and has been dead for a long time. My inference is further supported here where it says, "Gone were the rustlings of life, the blaze of color, and the birdsong."

background knowledge is applied to the text to justify their inferences. For each shared reading book, Mrs. Blake creates an anchor chart. She also creates graphic organizers based on the anchor charts that students can use when reading with her in guided reading, while working with partners, or when reading by themselves.

Guided Reading

Mrs. Blake's guided reading groups are often made up of students who struggle with the strategy. She invites the students to join her as they read leveled texts or even a story from the anthology from the core reading program. She asks the students to read to a certain point, and then they share their schema and evidence from the text to support the inferences they make and record this on graphic organizers. At other times, she sends the students to read the books with partners, and they come back and complete the graphic organizer together.

Independent Reading

While Mrs. Blake works with small groups of students in guided reading, other students read with partners or independently. During this time, students can choose any book they want to read. Some prefer to listen to themselves read through whisper phones, while others read quietly with partners or silently to themselves. These students complete either graphic organizers or write journal entries to keep records of their thinking. Two girls used the illustrations in *The Mystery of Harris Burdick* (Allsburg, 1984) to make inferences, and the Inferring From Text Graphic Organizer (see Appendix A) worked well for them to share their thinking. Students often make reference to the graphic organizers or journal entries in the whole-group sharing at the end of readers' workshop. Mrs. Blake observes that the student conversations in sharing are often insightful and have helped some students to better understand how to use the strategies in their reading.

Mrs. Blake reminds her students that inferring is a strategy that is always tied to other strategies. She emphasizes that good readers use all of their strategies and not just one at a time. Her students continue to practice previously taught strategies. Book choice is critical because not every book lends itself to every strategy. Often she sees that some of her students are a week or two behind her strategy instruction and gradually catch up. "Kids need to make discoveries on their own," she notes.

Other Strategies and Knowledge Applied to Independent Reading

Comprehension strategies and knowledge are not the only tools students apply while they are reading independently. Strategies related to vocabulary, fluency, story grammar for fiction, text structures for informational texts, and informational text features are often applied as well. Buly (2006) notes the following:

Independent reading provides the time for students to practice the important skills they have been taught in text with minimal challenges, which gives students success, a better chance of engagement, and hopefully the desire to reach for books when they are out of our sight. (p. 129)

Table 15 provides examples of other strategies and knowledge you can use to support students' independent reading.

Table 15. Modeling Comprehension, Vocabulary, Navigational Aids, Story Grammar, Text Structure, and Features of Informational Text for Elementary Readers

Components	Definition	Subtypes
Comprehension	Strategies to help understand text	Building background knowledge/making connections, constructing mental images, inferring, determining importance, predicting, summarizing/synthesizing, monitoring, evaluation
Vocabulary	Strategies for figuring out word meanings, not providing definitions	Affixes, root words, context clues, dictionary, inferring word meanings
Story grammar	Story elements found in fiction	Character, setting, goals or problems, events, themes, resolution
Text structures for informational text	Structures used in presenting information that readers can use to predict and process information	Compare and contrast, cause and effect, problem and solution, question and answer, description, chronological
Text features	Features of informational text	Boldfaced and italicized text, captions, tables, graphs, charts, diagrams, glossaries
Navigational devices	Informational text features that help readers find information and to see how the information is related to the structure of the text	Table of contents, index, page numbers, guide words, headings and subheadings

Note. Adapted from Duke, 2009; Fisher, Frey, & Lapp, 2008; Harvey & Goudvis, 2007; Keene, 2008; Mooney, 2001

Vocabulary

An important literacy goal is for students to develop as independent word learners (Blachowicz & Fisher, 2009). Teaching words prior to reading is necessary, but for independent reading students need to learn strategies to determine word meaning without your guidance. These strategies include using context clues, affixes, root words, dictionary skills, and inferring meanings of unknown words. Some of these strategies can be taught through word sorts although others need direct instruction through the GRR model.

Mrs. Blake's third-grade students learn to infer word meanings. An anchor chart posted in the classroom states in part,

> We are learning about inferring as a thinking strategy proficient readers use to better understand their reading. We infer the meanings of words by using the pictures, using our schema, the words in the text, rereading, thinking, and listening to others.

This chart serves as a reminder that inferring word meanings is important, and it describes how students can accomplish this task while reading. The following is an excerpt from one student's journal showing her thinking while trying to infer the meaning of the word *marauders* in Polacco's (1994) *Pink and Say.*

> At first I was thinking that marauders were people that hunt down black people and keep them for slaves.
>
> Then I thought marauders meant people that are from the other side of the war and they hunt down people from your own side.
>
> Now I'm thinking that marauders means people who hurt other people and take all their valuables and money.
>
> In the dictionary it says to raid for plunder, or to invade for loot.

The student's journal entry shows that she is well on her way to becoming a proficient reader because of her ability to infer the meaning of a word that is used infrequently in her oral and written language contexts.

Fluency

According to the NRP (NICHD, 2000), fluent reading involves readers reading with accuracy, speed, and ease so that a student's oral reading sounds like spoken language. The NRP also notes that fluency plays an important role in both the reading process and in reading instruction. Repeated oral reading was endorsed by the NRP for fostering fluency. However, Kuhn (2004; Kuhn & Schwanenflugel, 2009) found that increased silent reading practice often influenced students' reading fluency more quickly than repeated readings. Thus we suggest that you continue to involve your students in repeated reading activities such as Readers Theatre and choral reading and also make daily independent reading a key component of fluency building.

Story Grammar

Understanding narrative text structure is critical to students' comprehension of fiction. Generally we think of text structure as story grammar—the features found in stories. These features include setting, characters, character goals or problems, events to achieve the goal or to deal with the problem, theme, and a resolution. Dymock (2007) summarizes research related to story grammar instruction and notes several important points for teachers:

- Students with a good understanding of narrative text structure or story grammar have fewer problems comprehending narrative texts.
- Some students are able to figure out story grammar on their own, but others need explicit instruction.
- Even young students benefit from story grammar instruction.

There is a range in the degree of story grammar instruction and discussion across the grades. For instance, kindergarten and first-grade students recognize that Wilbur is the main character in White's (1952) classic *Charlotte's Web*. Fifth graders, on the other hand, can identify that Lucky is the protagonist in Patron's (2006) *The Higher Power of Lucky*, and that she is both a round and dynamic character.

Knowledge of story grammar elements is certainly relevant during independent reading. Students often complete character maps, story maps, plot graphs, and other activities in response to their readings. Such activities allow them to show their understanding of the literary elements and enhance their appreciation of the stories and books read.

Informational Text Structures

Authors of informational texts organize information in patterns such as compare and contrast, cause and effect, problem and solution, question and answer, chronological, and description. These patterns, known as text structures, typically use signal words that alert students to the structure employed. Graphic organizers and signal words are a good way to model for students how to recognize the structures and how to unpack information from reading informational texts. Students can then practice these strategies with guidance.

As with other strategies, Fisher, Frey, and Lapp (2008) note that exemplary teachers of older students typically teach these structures to their students through the shared reading approach. Dreher and Gray (2009) illustrate how one of the structures, compare and contrast, can be taught to young ELLs. Their graphic organizers can easily be adapted for use with older students as well. For modeling, begin with a blank compare-and-contrast graphic organizer and think aloud as you write on the organizer; a partially filled organizer can be used during guided reading, and you can provide a blank one for your students' use during independent reading (see Figure 4).

Figure 4. Compare and Contrast Structure Graphic Organizer for Modeling

As we read the text, compare and contrast the two animals: How are they alike? How are they different? Write down the ways that the animals are alike and different on this chart.

Alligators	Both	Crocodiles
Most have round snouts	Sharp teeth	Most have pointed snouts
Live only in the United States and China	Long tails	Live in many part of the world
Teeth do not stick out when their jaws are closed	Short legs Scaly skin	Teeth stick out when their jaws are closed

Note. Adapted from Dreher, M.J., & Gray, J.L. (2009). Compare, contrast, comprehend: Using compare-contrast text structures with ELLs in K–3 classrooms. *The Reading Teacher, 63*(2), 132–141.

Informational Text Features

Captions, diagrams, glossaries, tables, graphs, charts, and boldfaced and italicized words are examples of features that authors use in informational text. Students can readily find information when they understand how these features work. Many of the features are especially helpful in determining importance of information. For example, publishers often use italics or boldfaced print to signal that certain words are important. Thus, boldfaced and italicized print should alert students to pay careful attention while reading that section. Important facts are often reiterated in the nonnarrative portions of the text through tables, graphs, and charts. Teaching students to read and construct these features greatly enhances their learning with informational texts. Captions are often more than just labels for photos. Teaching students the different types and purposes of captions also helps them become independent learners.

Navigational Devices in Informational Text

Navigational devices, those components in informational text that enable readers to find information, help students to see how information fits within the structure and organization of the book. Understanding how these devices work helps students immensely in their reading of informational text and reinforces the notion that they do not have to read from cover to cover when learning with informational text.

Teachers model the various navigational devices in short minilessons. For example, Deb Glatt, a fourth-grade teacher in Washington, uses a document camera to show her students the index from Llewellyn's (2008) *Killer Creatures*. She begins by briefly explaining the purpose of an index and then models for the students how she uses it to quickly find information. She chooses "deathstalker scorpions" from the index, points out to students the page where she can find the information, turns to that page, scans for the specific information, and reads what she has found to them. Her students respond with "Ooh," and "Ah," and "That's so cool!" They beg her to read about the other scorpions on the two-page spread. She returns to the index and lets a student choose a topic of interest, and then asks another student about the page number where she can find the information. Again she turns to that page and reads the information to them. She continues this process two more times. This is enough practice that most students understand how to use the index. Her students are now begging to read the book.

Response to Reading Activities

We believe there are two purposes for student response to reading. First, response activities often deepen students' understanding and appreciation for the text read. Second, students are often motivated to read a book after observing the shared responses of their peers. Although we firmly believe in the value and power of students' response to reading, we believe that you must be intentional in how response activities are used in the classroom. First and foremost, we want students to spend most of their time reading. We know of instances where students have created elaborate models or detailed paintings that required more time than reading the book. We believe that a response should never take more than 20% of the time spent reading (Routman, 2003).

It's important to remember not to force students to submit a formal response to every book they read independently. Stead (2009) notes, "Responses to literature need to be fueled by the learners' wonderings, surprises, and connections. Responses need to be driven by the readers' passion and not a list of questions that becomes a blueprint for all responses" (p. 150). Response activities can be exciting and pleasurable for students when they have some choice in which books they respond to and how they respond. Requiring students to respond to every book becomes tedious and removes any possible joy the students may have experienced.

Responding With Art

Many elementary students prefer using art to respond to their reading over writing and discussion because they perceive it as more fun. Hancock (2008) emphasizes that art response activities "must lie within the literature itself rather than being artificially attached to a book" (p. 339). The following ideas can help students respond with art.

Illustrator Study. Students can read multiple picture books by the same illustrator and then try their hand at using some of the same techniques as the illustrator (Hancock, 2008). For example, a student might read books illustrated by Carle—such as *Dragons, Dragons and Other Creatures*

That Never Were (Carle, 1999), *"Slowly, Slowly, Slowly" Said the Sloth* (Carle, 2002), or *Mister Seahorse* (Carle, 2004)—and carefully study his illustrations. The student could then use simple shapes of tissue paper and painted paper to create illustrations similar to Carle's.

Collage. Geoffrey read Napoli's (2010) *Mama Miti: Wangari Maathai and the Trees of Kenya* and found himself charmed with both Wangari Maathai's Green Belt Movement to plant trees in Kenya and with Kadir Nelson's stunning illustrations. Geoffrey decided to create a collage to compare Wangari Maathai with Johnny Appleseed. Where Kadir Nelson utilized printed fabrics and oil paints to illustrate *Mama Miti,* Geoffrey used scrapbooking paper in his collage. His work illustrated a text-to-text connection he made between two people who literally changed the landscape of their nations.

Puppetry. Darya, a fourth grader, was delighted to read *Baba Yaga and Vasilisa the Brave* retold by Mayer (1994) and reconnect with a story she had heard in Russia before moving to the United States. She created puppets (as pictured in Figure 5) so she could retell the story to the

Figure 5. Darya's Puppets

Russian and Ukrainian children in her school. Her response to reading activity combined both art and drama as she shared the tale with younger students in her school.

Responding With Drama

Drama is often underused in many elementary schools. Yet it has great potential in advancing student literacy and is quite enjoyable as well. Adomat (2009) notes that drama "not only helps children to understand story elements and structure more deeply through multiple character roles over time, but also it allows for a personalized interpretation of text" (p. 633). Researchers have noted that drama is beneficial to all students including struggling readers (Adomat, 2009) and ELLs (Hadaway et al., 2002). There are many ways in which students can use drama to respond to literature read during independent reading; a small sampling follows.

Choral Reading. After you introduce various choral reading arrangements (e.g., refrain, two voices, antiphonal/call and response, cumulative) a student can arrange a poem or poems for choral reading (Hadaway, Vardell, & Young, 2006). The student then leads a group of his or her classmates in the performance of the reading. This is a very appropriate way for students to respond to a poetry collection or anthology.

Hot Seat. Another dramatic response to reading is hot seat, which is especially effective when a group of students have read a common book. One teacher used this approach after a group of her students read the final chapter of Broach's (2008) *Masterpiece*. Those students came up with two questions that they would ask the buyer for the gallery, Marvin, James, and James's father if those characters were present. Next the teacher invited students to take on those roles. The selected students' responses to questions had to stay in the context of the book and in the voice of the character. Classmates then asked the questions the readers had prepared in advance. This gave the other students a glimpse into the book, and the participants felt that their individual interpretations were strengthened as they thought through their answers and listened to the responses of their peers. Adomat (2009) describes how hot seat was used with first graders who had listened to *Owen* by Henkes (1993).

Readers Theatre. Teachers find that watching a Readers Theatre presentation based on a portion of a book often motivates students to read the book in its entirety. You can capitalize on the motivational nature of Readers Theatre by having older students prepare and perform the scripts on books they have read. Readers Theatre has been shown to have many benefits for students—especially in terms of fluency (see Young & Rasinski, 2009). Readers Theatre is frequently considered for fiction, but Young and Vardell (1993) suggest that Readers Theatre scripts based on nonfiction motivate students and reinforce the curriculum.

Responding With Writing

Most teachers and researchers readily recognize that writing is a wonderful way to think about and respond to their reading. Yet few leaders in the field recommend the use of book reports; in fact, they uniformly discourage their use.

Teachers find various types of journals and writing notebooks useful for their students' response to reading. Some take the form of a letter the students write to the teacher who in turn responds to them. Miller (2009) notes,

> These letters are exchanges between a more experienced reader and a less experienced reader, not a list of questions probing whether or not [the student] read the book. I challenge [the student] to think more deeply about the book, but from the stance of a more advanced reader who read *Inkheart* (Funke, 2003), too. Readers whispering back and forth about their reading experiences—this is how reading should look. (p. 102)

Students also enjoy other types of short writing responses, such as the following.

Book Reviews. Student book reviews are authentic ways in which students in grade 3 and higher can write about the books they read. You can teach students about the book review genre by reading sample reviews to analyze the components of a good review. Miller (2009) requires the following elements in book reviews from her students:

- Quotes from the book
- Personal reactions and opinions
- Recommended reading age
- Awards the book or author has won
- Other books by the same author
- Comparisons with other books

Writing book reviews gives students an opportunity to share with other readers what they love about the books they have read (Miller, 2009).

Poetry. Sometimes students deeply relate to a book they have read and feel compelled to write a poem in response to it. Such was the case with Alejandro, a fifth-grade student whose mother was an immigrant from Mexico. He read Bunting's (1998) *Going Home* and responded by writing the poem in Figure 6 about his family's feelings about their separation from loved ones in Mexico and their identity with two countries. Alejandro's poem reflects the powerful text-to-self connection that he made with Bunting's book.

Figure 6. Alejandro's Poem

The Two Sides
When I was little, My mother would say,
"I wish your uncle could come!"
And she'd sigh.
"Who is my uncle," I'd ask.
"He is wonderful, delightful man,"
She would say,
and her eyes would fill up with tears,
And her face would frown.
"Can I go to see him," I'd ask,
And mom would look up and say,
"It's so far."
"How far?" I wouldn't give up.
"It is like two sides of the world.
My brother is on one side
And we are far away
On the other side.
You'll see him
Some other time."
She'd whisper.
"No, I want to see him now,
My sides are both sides,"
I said, and mom looked at me.
And she knew I was going to go…
She let me go during winter break
To see my uncle because
She realized that I DO have
Two equally important sides
And that I don't give up easily.

Another poetry response might be creating found poems, in which students can select words, lines, and phrases from a chapter that they think projects strong images about a character or some other aspect of a book. These can then be arranged into a poem (Mitchell, 1998). The found poem in Figure 7 was written by Kadi. She focused her poem on Harry Potter's wand and based it on lines and phrases from Rowling's (1998) *Harry Potter and the Sorcerer's Stone*.

Mitchell (1998) recommends the title acrostic in which students write the title down the side of a piece of construction paper. For each letter in the title, they then write a sentence that begins with that letter telling something significant about the book. Figure 8 shows a title acrostic, created by Vicki, for Anderson's (2008) *Chains*.

Figure 7. Kadi's Found Poem

The Wand Chooses the Wizard

Curious
Curious indeed
How things happen.
The wand chooses the wizard
Remember
Every wand ever sold
Holly and phoenix feather
Eleven inches
The wand chooses the wizard
We must expect great things
From you, Mr. Potter.
He-Who-Must-Not-Be-Named
Did great things.
Terrible,
But great.
The wand chooses the wizard

Figure 8. Vicki's Title Acrostic

Craack! was the sound that echoed off buildings as Mistress slapped Isabel's face.
Hatred was a concept Isabel experienced first-hand as the chattel of her owners.
Ad astra was the code word that gave Isabel admittance to the rebel camp.
I was the letter branded on Isabel's cheek as punishment for insolence to her mistress.
Night was the cover Isabel and Curzon needed for their escape from New York.
Slavery was not considered a moral issue even though the rebels were fighting for
    "liberty and freedom."

Responding With Technology

Kelly Killorn, a sixth-grade teacher in Bloomington, Minnesota, who was named the 2009 winner of IRA's Award for Technology and Reading, explains how her students use technology during and after reading to strengthen their comprehension and response to reading. She notes that technology has great appeal to and benefits for her students. She finds that technology is not only fun for them but also motivating to reluctant readers, aids all of her students in their attempts to comprehend text, helps them organize their thinking, and enhances their learning. Yet the major benefit to using technology is that it provides students with an authentic audience besides their teacher and classmates.

Students who are struggling readers especially benefit from using technology while reading. Ms. Killorn loads the popular books that more advanced students are reading onto MP3 players, and the students listen to the text while following along in the book. This allows struggling students to experience the text, which allows them to discuss and respond to books that they otherwise would not be able to read. Their responses indicate that they are just as capable of thinking about the books as their peers.

She believes that many of her students feel more comfortable in discussing books online than they do in class discussions. They often feel a sense of security being in front of a computer monitor instead of in face-to-face discussions. The online forum gives students more time to think through and edit their responses, and it provides them with opportunities to interact with students in other classes about the books they are reading. She feels the quality of her students' online responses are much more thoughtful and deeper than what students might share orally in class. The following examples demonstrate some of the ways that Ms. Killorn's students respond to the books that they read.

Book Advertisements. Book advertisements are like commercials for a book read by a small group of five students. Each student has a role in these cooperative projects. The roles include script writing, designing a backdrop, selecting music to accompany the production, finding an appropriate video clip to include, and editing the video in the computer lab. Students take great pride in their work and few people would guess that sixth graders actually do all the work themselves. "The students are amazing when it comes to what they can do with technology," Ms. Killorn says. "Many times the students exceed my expectations on a project or an assignment because they enjoy the work so much."

Wikis. The wiki provides students with a space where they can respond to questions regarding the books they are reading as part of a genre study. Ms. Killorn's students blog entries as book characters and post video diaries (like those seen on a reality television show) in the wiki. The video diaries are made using FLIP cameras. Her students note that the video diaries help them visualize the characters in the book and to focus on those characters' problems and goals. Ms. Killorn observes that the student blog postings and video diaries are a great way to motivate others to read the books that their classmates have chosen. (A quick Internet search will give you access to instructions for starting a wiki.)

Message Boards. Ms. Killorn uses a ning (www.ning.com) to create a secure message board that is much like the popular social networking sites MySpace and Facebook. She notes that she never requires her students to use technology at home because not all students have access to the Internet. Yet she finds that there are always some kids logged in and having fun with things that are directly related to school and the books they are reading. "That can only be a good thing," she notes. (A quick Internet search will give you access to instructions for creating a ning.)

Gambrell (2009) notes that today's teachers are no longer expected to read silently with their students during independent reading. Instead teachers talk about what they are reading, and this talk becomes an important model of reading purposes and behaviors. Ms. Killorn accomplishes this through the blog she keeps of her own reading. Her students, in turn, can earn extra credit for reading books on her blog and then posting a review of each book read.

Monitoring and Assessing Student Response

Just as students sometimes fall into ruts and only want to read one genre or series of books, they often want to respond to all of the books they read through art or drama (Stead, 2009). While choice is always important, sometimes you need to nudge students to try a variety of response to reading activities. Many resources have examples of reading logs and checklists for monitoring both students' reading and their response to reading (e.g., Hancock, 2008; Stead, 2009). We can learn a lot about students through their records of the books they read and their responses to reading. Yet Hancock (2008) reminds us that literature response assessment must be both quantitative and qualitative: "In other words, keeping track of numbers of books and responses is important, but this must be supplemented by data on quality and depth of response and the various literature experiences" (p. 417).

IRA and the National Council of Teachers of English's (NCTE) Joint Task Force on Assessment (IRA/NCTE, 1994) developed standards for literacy assessment. Using those standards as a foundation, Hancock (2008) created the following guidelines for assessing response-based celebrations of literature.

- Literature tastes and response-based preferences of students are paramount in assessment.
- The primary purpose of response-based assessment is to improve teaching and learning.
- Response-based assessments must recognize and reflect the intellectual and social complexity of literacy and the role of school, home, and society in literacy development.
- The teacher is the most important agent of response-based assessment.
- The response-based assessment process should involve multiple perspectives and sources of data.
- Parents should be involved as active, essential participants in a response-based process. (pp. 419–420)

Hancock (2008) not only provides guidelines for response-based assessment but also has rubrics, graphs, charts, checklists, teacher prompts, and a taxonomy of response to reading to guide you in assessing students' response journals and other response activities. As we carefully analyze students' response to reading, we can plan appropriate instruction to help them find increased joy, appreciation, and understanding in the books they read.

One fourth-grade teacher taught her students to evaluate their literature response notebooks by having them use colored pencils to shade their responses according to categories. The teacher wanted to move the students beyond retelling plots. Students used yellow for plot retellings, purple for text-to-text connections, red for text-to-self connections, blue for predictions or inferences about upcoming events in the book, green for responses that reflect reader response to a character, and orange for what they students considered their deepest text response. She found that with lots of modeling and student sharing, her students increased their types of response to reading and their notebooks were no longer only repositories of plot retellings.

Likewise a fifth-grade teacher made copies of many of her former students' response to reading activities and created a bulletin board where she categorized the responses as Novice Response, Emerging Response, Maturing Response, or Self-Directed Response (all names were removed from the responses). She could use the bulletin board as a tool to teach the current year's students more about how to deepen their responses to reading. As her students shared their response to reading pieces in conferences, she would have them explain where they would place their responses on the bulletin board and justify their placements. The teacher found that each year's students demonstrated deeper and more quality response to reading pieces because of the previous year's anonymous sample responses available on the bulletin board and the discussions about them.

It is necessary to scaffold instruction so that your students can apply the strategies they learned to their independent reading. Strategies are modeled, taught, and practiced using a GRR, providing reading to, with, and by students. This model allows for students to learn strategies while working in large groups, small groups, with partners, and individually. Likewise provide your students with instruction and opportunities to respond to their reading through writing, drama, art, music, and technology. Student responses are monitored through conferences and student record keeping to ensure the students select a variety of response types and that the responses actually strengthen student understanding and appreciation of the books read.

Sharon Taberski is well known throughout North America for her work as a teacher, a consultant, and a staff development trainer. She is the author of the popular book *On Solid Ground: Strategies for Teaching Reading K–3* and the DVD set *It's ALL About Comprehension: Teaching K-3 Readers From the Ground Up*. Taberski also has a forthcoming book about teaching comprehension in the early grades.

Terrell Young: What is your best advice for teachers for creating independent readers and learners?

Sharon Taberski: My best advice to teachers for developing independent readers and learners is to confer with students. I know it takes a lot of time and very often teachers can't imagine how they can possibly work with students one on one when they have so much else to do. Yet to me, it's the most important thing. You have to know your students so you can respond to them in ways that make a difference and direct them toward the right reading materials and the skills and strategies they need to learn. The guidance and feedback you provide during reading conferences is invaluable and paves the way for a more effective independent reading time.

Teachers should also recognize that students can only attend to something that's moderately stressful—as learning to read most certainly is—for short amounts of time. Basically, the number of minutes matches their age: if they're 7 years old, they can read for approximately seven minutes; 5 years old, five minutes; 9 years old, nine minutes. This doesn't mean that we stop independent reading after seven, five, or nine minutes and give the kids worksheets to do. It just means that we have to factor in some downtime experiences, like Readers Theatre, partner reading, reading responses, discussions, reading log work, and strategy sheets. And then have students read some more.

We mustn't expect our independent reading times of day to be as quiet as we'd like. That's not going to happen when you're talking about students reading on their own for extended periods of time. Nor is it advisable when they're novice readers just starting out. These readers need to subvocalize. And all readers need to interact. Even when they're on task, the room is bound to be filled with a lot of noise-related learning: discussing books, reading together, reading alone, and not the silence that was typical of the kind of independent reading to which we aspired years ago. This is definitely not uninterrupted SSR. (And that's a good thing.) It looks very different and it sounds different, too.

So all and all, there's a lot teachers can do to build stamina and increase the amount of independent reading students do. And yet they must also recognize that in the middle of it all, they're going to need to stand up several times and simply tell students to "stop it." This is part of the dance.

TY: During guided reading, some teachers keep their students dependent upon them and their support to complete the task at hand. What advice would you give to those teachers?

ST: Much of what I do during guided reading depends on the age and grade of the students, and the length, difficulty, and type of book we're reading. The ultimate goal is to release more responsibility to the students. So, in this small group, I want to give students more responsibility than I might in a whole-class setting but less than I would when I send them off to work on their own.

This means that I may direct students to read a portion of the text and then stop them to discuss how it went, what they learned, and what's happening. Or if I'm working with emergent readers who are reading an eight-page text, I might walk them through the entire book and then say, "Now go ahead and read." I think that if you keep in mind the release-of-responsibility model and what you've set out to demonstrate, your specific interactions with students during guided reading will take shape naturally and reflect your goals.

TY: Sometimes teachers put so much emphasis on comprehension strategies that the strategies take on a life of their own. As a result, students are more focused on applying a strategy than trying to understand the text. How can teachers avoid this?

ST: First of all, I'm convinced that there needs to be a schoolwide approach to comprehension strategy instruction where, throughout the course of the elementary grades, students acquire a repertoire of comprehension strategies and understand that strategies are to be used if, and as, needed. The "if-and-as-needed" message should be made loud and clear because, as you know, all too often strategies have taken center stage, to the point where teachers are interrupting students' reading (and their comprehension) by asking them to stop and do things that are unnecessary. This is not how it works, and we don't want students to get the wrong message.

There should be less focus on comprehension strategy instruction, per se, and more on other facets of literacy that are equal contributors to students' developing ability to comprehend. Background knowledge, reading–writing connections, accurate fluent reading, and oral language and vocabulary are *as important* as the strategies themselves. As things stand right now, the strategies are given top billing while others areas of comprehension are pushed to the side.

Don't get me wrong. Comprehension strategies *are* important, and they do play a role in students' learning to read and comprehend. But at they moment, they're being overdone. As a result we're making comprehension teaching and learning more complex than it needs to be.

Let me explain how I think this schoolwide approach to comprehension strategy instruction, that I mentioned earlier, should play out. The first step is for schools to identify the metacognitive strategies they want students to acquire by the time they leave fifth grade and make this known to all the teachers. That way, teachers across the grades will know the goal and can determine how to do their developmentally appropriate part to achieve it.

Next, the three facets of this approach come into play. In kindergarten and first grade there should be a strong emphasis on student reading, writing, and talking—experiences that facilitate comprehension learning rather than teach it directly. Teachers can expose students to meaning-making strategies by thinking aloud about what they do as readers and naming the strategies, but they shouldn't require students to go off and do most of these things on their own. Not yet. Laura Smolkin and Carol Donovan's (2000) research jumpstarted my thinking in this regard because they differentiated between comprehension *acquisition* and comprehension *learning* and say there's a time and place for both throughout elementary-grade schooling.

In second and third grade, I recommend focus strategy units. This is where the heavy-duty strategy demonstrations and guided practice kick in. Now the students are old enough to really understand what the teacher is after, and they can try these strategies out and come back to the group to process how it went. Here the second- and third-grade teachers divide the strategies between them, each taking half and developing a two-to-three week unit around each strategy. Then during the time between units, they provide authentic reading, writing, and talking experiences where students are building background knowledge, developing their vocabulary, making reading–writing connections, and so on. They're all important and all done to serve comprehension.

Then in fourth and fifth grade, the focus should shift from teaching a strategy in isolation to integrating them and helping students identify when and how to use them. That's the tricky part—knowing when meaning has broken down and deciding which of the strategies in your repertoire would be most helpful.

TY: How do you recommend that teachers address strategies in their independent reading conferences?

ST: To be quite honest, I don't think much about comprehension strategies one way or another during conferences. When I meet with students, I'm just trying to see how they're doing and how I can move them along. It may involve a comprehension strategy or it might not. For example, if I see that a student is struggling to read the words, and only attending to letter–sounds without using the picture cues, I explain how he should use letters–sounds and the pictures together. If I note that the passage a student is reading evokes a powerful image and begs to be visualized, I might point that out and help him consider how this affects his comprehension.

But what I don't typically do, which I know a lot of other teachers do or at least try to do, is insist that during independent reading students follow through with what I've demonstrated during a minilesson. That's hard, and I guess I've never really gotten my act together to the point where I can be sure that I've provided the right kinds of reading materials so that each of the readers in my class can actually try what I'm showing them. With such a wide range of readers within each class that's really hard. It sounds good in theory, but it's hard to implement.

On the other hand, there are times, during a focus strategy unit or a genre unit, for example, where I'll demonstrate a strategy and direct students to go off and practice it, and then come back to talk about what they did. It's during those times and during those conferences where I'm curious to see how students are applying a specific strategy and whether it's helpful.

TY: After the NRP report, many people have suggested that independent reading should take place outside of school. What is your response to that suggestion?

ST: I think that, in this instance, the NRP report has been misinterpreted. Or at least I hope that's the case. It's my understanding that the report questions the effectiveness of independent reading when it's done *without teacher guidance and feedback*. The type of independent reading that I'm recommending most definitely factors in both guidance and feedback.

When I meet with students for conferences, I match them with just right books and other texts that will engage them. I determine what they're doing well and might do better and share this information with them. I write students notes in their assessment notebook about what they might try during independent reading. When we gather for guided reading, I guide them through a text, scaffolding their reading, and then give them the book to keep in their book bag to read on their own. I sometimes give them a companion text (one that complements the guided reading selection in terms of strategy, theme, or genre) that will give students something new, but related, to read.

Although I'm confident that my independent reading practices do provide students with guidance and feedback, I'm always trying to get better in this regard. Independent reading is too important to have it any other way.

To say or imply that "independent reading" may not be an effective use of school time and recommend that it take place at home would be irresponsible. And I don't think that's what the NRP report intended to imply. What about the kids who don't have books at home, or whose home environments aren't conducive to reading? And what about kids who don't like to read and don't read well? They need time to read *in school* under the guidance and supervision of a teacher who knows what books they should be reading and is able to guide them.

TY: What do you view as the role of instruction during independent reading time?

ST: The instruction occurs by way of the environment I create, the materials I provide, and the strategies and skills I demonstrate throughout read-aloud, shared reading, reading conferences, small-group work, and writing. (Let's not forget writing because there's a definite connection between the writing students do and their ability to read and comprehend text.)

The environment in which reading and learning occur and the materials I provide for students to read are so important. The classroom has to be relaxing and engaging, full of nooks and crannies for students to snuggle up in and read. You know, or at least I hope you know, that I don't mean having students lie down or that kind of thing. But their learning environment still needs to be comfortable, unlike those that I see in so many schools where students are sitting poker-straight at their desks reading their books and trying to be "silent." In addition, the books and other reading materials need to be supportive, yet engaging. There are so many wonderful choices for teachers these days. I advise them to take the time to see what trade books are out there and bring some fabulous ones into the classroom, and peruse the publisher's catalog to find the very best of the best. Our students deserve it.

Throughout the reading workshop or, if you prefer, balanced literacy, I demonstrate what good readers do and then, during independent reading, I give them time and invite them to try out some of these skills and strategies on their own. This balance of explicit instruction and time to practice is what it's all about. Instruction without time to practice won't work; neither will time to read without explicit instruction. They're both part of what it means to read and learn, and it's our job to strike the right balance.

CHAPTER 5

Independent Reading in the Content Area Classroom

Early in her teaching career, the first author learned firsthand about the appeal of content-related trade books to young readers. She began teaching more than 30 years ago, working with struggling readers in grades 5–8 in a rural northeastern Ohio school district. Her students were predominantly male, caught in that murky purgatory known as adolescence. Reading was low on their list of favorite activities. It was something they did in school, but only under duress.

As a novice teacher, she knew little about the technical aspects of reading instruction but did know the critical importance of getting students to *want* to read. She fervently believed, and still does, that by providing students with books about topics of passionate personal interest she could lure them into the "literacy club." As her professor at Kent State University, Carl Rosen, noted, children are curious creatures and that curiosity can be the catalyst that transforms a reluctant reader into a lifelong one. Hearne (2000) says it best: "In the matter of education, a child's own curiosity is the greatest tool. It starts long before school does and is a driving force in growing up" (p. 155). This curiosity often sparks learning that persists well beyond the elementary years—and sometimes continues throughout a lifetime.

She soon discovered that the topics her students wanted to read about were not ones that held much fascination for her. The books they selected from the meager classroom library during SSR time were almost exclusively factual in content. Biographies about famous athletes and informational titles about rocks, first aid, dinosaurs, war, fishing, and football flew off the shelves. These books fueled the students' curiosity and answered their questions about the universe—about the people, places, and things they encountered in their daily lives. Despite the difficulty of these books and their less-than-enticing appearances, her students would read them and engage with the pictures, asking questions like, "Did you know that fish can swim backwards?" This led to talk surrounding these texts, regular sharing of books, and a general increase in enthusiasm for reading.

Regardless of a student's area of interest, whether rocks and minerals, horses, dinosaurs, medieval weaponry, outer space, or art, this curiosity about the world can provide a natural starting point for engagement with books in the content area classroom. In this chapter, we describe how you can capitalize on your students' curiosity about the real world to create independent reading experiences that engage and motivate content learning.

A Rationale for Independent Reading in the Content Areas

Today's content area classrooms continue to be dominated by textbook use despite the increasing availability of other options such as trade books and electronic media. For some students, the only historical, mathematics, or science materials they will ever read in a lifetime are in textbooks. Out of necessity, textbooks provide breadth about topics like science and social studies, but they provide little depth. Trade books and other texts offer in-depth information about content-related topics and perspectives that may have been excluded from textbooks. Learning with trade books and other texts exposes students to many different genres and forms, all of which are potential sources of knowledge. When you use trade books along with textbooks, you help learners think critically about content as well as consider the larger questions of the world.

Although independent reading is not often found in content area classrooms, it should be. Independent reading can provide unique advantages in teaching students the content of history, health, science, mathematics, art, or music. Independent reading can do the following:

- Help differentiate instruction by meeting the range of reading levels in the classrooms. By using a variety of trade books at different levels, you can match students with books they can read. This allows you the opportunity to give students books at their independent reading levels, a practice that has been associated with gains in achievement.

- Provide time on task for content area learning. Content area learning is receiving far less attention in today's classrooms than in the past because of the emphasis on reading and mathematics resulting from federal and state testing requirements. Seventy-one percent of districts nationwide have reduced time spent on subjects other than reading and mathematics (Jennings & Rentner, 2006). Independent reading of content-related texts can provide additional exposure to content area learning beyond that provided during the school day.

- Give students much-needed practice in reading informational texts, which are typically less familiar to students than narratives and more difficult for them to read. The ability to read expositions, argumentation and persuasive texts, and procedural texts and documents require different skills, but all are critical to reading and understanding across content subjects (Saul, 2006). Many students do not know how to read to learn with informational texts because their school experiences have been limited to textbook-only reading. Independent reading in the content area classroom can expose students to a range of informational genres, thereby increasing student facility with a range of text types.

- Motivate students to read to learn. The compelling qualities of today's content-related books, for example, make them many students' favorite out-of-school reading. Authors of today's informational trade books not only provide information but also entertain readers in ways that make information engaging. Through this engagement in content area topics, students increase their reading volume, which is associated with improved reading.

The mastery of content area materials requires at least three key components: (1) domain knowledge about the content area, (2) knowledge and understanding of discipline specific vocabulary, and (3) understanding of oral and written discourse forms unique to the discipline. Take for example the study of science. It, like all content areas, demands a particular way of thinking, talking, and writing about the world. Success in learning science, or any content area, is dependent on the development of domain knowledge. This deep knowledge about a particular topic requires long-term immersion in an area of study, and it enhances vocabulary understanding as well as comprehension. It is an absolute requirement for reading comprehension (Hirsch, 2003).

Success in learning science also depends upon vocabulary knowledge. Science possesses its own specific vocabulary that, because it is unlike everyday language, poses unique challenges to students. As Cervetti, Pearson, Bravo, and Barber (2006) note, "Scientists make predictions rather than guesses, they observe rather than see, and they talk about habitats rather than homes and properties rather than qualities" (p. 237).

To succeed in the science classroom, students also need to understand and be able to comprehend those discourse forms unique to scientific learning, including the language of argumentation, hypothesis testing, cause and effect, and many other linguistic forms. In addition, students must learn to write using modes of discourse unique to this discipline. By reading books that model these forms, including explanations of processes, observational records, and so on, students are provided with models for their own writing.

What does independent reading have to do with the development of these critical skills? Reading *widely* about a topic from a range of texts can deepen students' domain knowledge in important ways. Trade books, magazines, and electronic texts about a particular topic "leave in the child's mind a residue of information about people, times, places, processes, and heroes" (Montabello, 1972, p. 63). By exploring topics through trade books, students develop a rich context for understanding many aspects of a time, place, or phenomenon, thus enhancing their schema.

Social studies trade books like *The Queen's Progress: An Elizabethan Alphabet* (Mannis, 2003) can contribute to the development of this domain knowledge through text and illustration. This lavishly illustrated alphabet book familiarizes students with the annual custom of the royal progress of the Queen, a lengthy trip around the country during which the she visited her subjects throughout the realm. It portrays typical amusements of the time, including dancing bears, Morris dancers, elaborate feasts, pageants, fox hunting, and jousting. It accurately portrays the clothing customs of the time for both villagers and the royal retinue and vividly depicts the English countryside, castles, gardens, and the like. More than just a pretty picture book, however, it explores the political aspects of the Queen's reign, describing through text and illustrations the many plots against the Queen's life. It clearly explains the dangers associated with these intrigues, identifying the daily precautions necessary to prevent harm to the Queen.

In addition to domain knowledge, *The Queen's Progress* familiarizes students with the terms and concepts associated with Elizabethan England. Replete with references to places like Hampton Court, the Tower of London, and the Thames, this book contextualizes these locations. Terms like *maze, hedgerows, nobles, crossbows, jester, tournament, lance, bedchamber, divine rights,* and *zounds* familiarize students with academic language associated with this time period.

Finally, *The Queen's Progress* familiarizes students with the expository discourse form of description, which is often found in social studies texts. Interestingly, though, the description is embedded in an alphabet, providing a text structure students have experienced since the very early grades.

Selecting Books for Independent Reading in the Content Areas

As you will recall, we discussed the topic of book selection at length in Chapter 2 and gave some ideas for focus lessons on book selection in Chapter 3. However, when considering independent reading in the content areas, we feel that it is important to offer additional suggestions for selecting titles for social studies and science. Teachers often lack background knowledge in content area topics (Kiefer et al., 2006) and as a result may be unaware of the limitations of some titles. Second, book reviews of such titles can often be misleading because reviewers too may have expertise in terms of literary quality but lack knowledge about content. The following sections discuss genres suited to these content areas and offer book selection guidelines for both content areas.

Selecting Books for the Social Studies Classroom

Biographies, historical fiction, and informational trade books are especially popular in the social studies classroom. Biographies can help people from the past and present come alive, allowing students to identify with real figures of significance. Both younger and older students can appreciate the combination of text and illustrations in picture book biographies. Single biographies like *Diego* (Winter, 2007), for example, focus on the life of one individual, in this case the life of the Mexican artist Diego Rivera. Collective biographies describe several subjects within the covers of a single book. Partial biographies like *Abe Lincoln Crosses a Creek: A Tall, Thin Tale* (Hopkinson, 2008) focus on a particular time or specific event in a subject's life, while cradle-to-grave biographies describe a subject's life from birth to death.

Historical fiction can be an indispensable resource in the social studies classroom because it tells a fictitious story embedded in a historical setting. The characters in the book are usually fictional, but may be based on people who actually lived. Historical information is (or should be) completely accurate, whether in describing the clothing of the period or in the kind of language used. Through historical fiction, students learn about the crises faced by people in the past, the enduring nature of people's basic needs, and the ways in which we depend on each other. Moreover, these books can describe the worst and best in human behavior through their revelations about those who have shaped history, both famous and not-so-famous. For example, in the 1989 Newbery Award-winning book *Number the Stars* (Lowry, 1989), students learn about the worst in human behavior through the actions of the Nazis, along with the best as Annemarie's family shelters her Jewish friend.

Informational trade books can promote student's understanding of all categories of social studies knowledge, present multiple perspectives, promote understanding of the past, and—where appropriate—present primary source materials. Many informational books emphasize a global perspective, helping students develop greater appreciation for the other cultures represented on our planet. *What the World Eats* (D'Aluisio, 2008) uses a photographic essay format to profile families across the globe and describe what they eat during one week. Each profile provides information about each family's food and its cost, a world map showing where each family lives, and facts about each country. The book describes families who fish for their food as well as those who obtain it in more conventional ways.

While many of the criteria for selecting books can be applied to social studies books, consider the following additional questions:

- Does the book represent diverse groups and depict a range of cultural experiences?
- Does the book provide a unique approach to a common topic?
- Is the book of high literary quality?
- Is the book appealing to students?
- Is the book accurate? Have the authors cited the sources from which they obtained their information?

- Are visuals (e.g., maps, graphs, charts, photographs) clear and easy to read? Are they accurate?
- Does the book provide current information on the topic?

Selecting Books for the Science Classroom

Quality science trade books can introduce students to scientific domains, present concepts and facts to students, describe the work of scientists, and model scientific processes and discourses. Science related biographies, reference books, informational books, narrative nonfiction and experiment books are a few of the types of texts that can help to achieve these goals. Science related biographies can engage students in learning about how scientific discoveries have been made and how human beings pursue the work of science. *Giants of Science: Marie Curie* (Krull, 2009), for example, details the difficulties of the human enterprise of scientific discovery in an easy-to-read text. Reference books like *Animal Tracks and Signs* (Johnson, 2009) exemplify the best of the many types of field guides available today. This book uses text, photographs, diagrams, and illustrations to help students identify hundreds of different types of animals. Narrative nonfiction titles like *Surtsey: The Newest Place on Earth* (Lasky, 2001), for example, illustrate the actual work of scientists as they observe, measure, and classify information. This title provides a model for students to use as they engage in scientific inquiry in their own classrooms. In addition, titles like *Surtsey* encourage students to think like scientists as they also observe, weigh evidence, and draw conclusions. Informational titles like Pringle's (2001) *Global Warming: The Threat of Earth's Changing Climate*, for example, use color illustrations, maps, graphs, and compelling text to not only explain the processes surrounding global warming, but also to increase student awareness of its ramifications for the world at large.

An important consideration in selecting science books is whether the books present misconceptions, supply erroneous information, or are confusing (Rice, Dudley, & Williams, 2001). In addition to the criteria for selecting books presented in Chapter 2, consider the following items specifically related to science:

- Does the book contain significant science content, and is it accurate?
- Is scientific inquiry addressed adequately through examples?

- Does the science content allow students to connect with their own experiences?

- Is the science content appropriate to the audience?

- Does the author distinguish between facts and theories?

- Are illustrations accurate and clear?

- Are scientists portrayed as real people engaged in the work of science?

Components of Independent Reading in the Content Areas

As we noted in Chapter 3, an independent reading program in the language arts includes two key components, 20 minutes of community reading time twice a week and 60 minutes of SIRT daily. Generally speaking, you use reading/language arts time for these two activities and, in a perfect world, would make time for independent reading during the language arts block *and* during content area instruction for one subject. However, there are many ways that you might carve out class time to focus on independent reading in the content area classroom The model of choice would depend on what was being studied and the time available. Here are three suggestions:

1. *The Additive Model*—This model involves expanding the independent reading program from the language arts classroom to include one or more content areas. In the language arts classroom, community reading time takes place for 20 minutes twice weekly, and SIRT occurs for 60 minutes daily during the language arts block. Using the additive model, you would continue the independent reading program during the language arts block and *extend* it into a content area. Community reading time, for example, might occur 20 minutes twice a week during social studies, science, art, or music, and SIRT would occur twice a week for 60 minutes during one of these content areas.

2. *The Integrated Model*—With this model, content area independent reading is integrated into reading/language arts time. For example, during specified blocks of time during each grading period, content

area related reading motivation activities would occur during reading language arts community reading time. SIRT during the language arts block would be devoted to minilessons and reading materials related to a given content area.

3. *The Combination Model*—With this model, you might use the additive model at certain points during the year and the integrated model at other times. For example, you might elect to have independent reading during the language arts block at the beginning of the year and then move it into a content area class during the study of a particular topic or unit. This flexible format could occur throughout the year, allowing you to incorporate independent reading into the content area classroom on an as-needed basis.

Community Reading Time

We believe at least 20 minutes twice a week should be devoted to increasing student motivation for reading within particular content areas. Through these experiences, students develop a deeper and a keener interest in content learning and the understanding that content area learning includes more than just the information that is found in a textbook; it encompasses a wide range of topics found in books in a variety of genres. Many of the suggestions for community reading time suggested in Chapter 3 can easily apply to the content area classroom. In this section, we discuss how book talks and interactive read-alouds can be adapted to the content area classroom community reading time, as well as discuss other activities appropriate to a content focus.

Book Talks. During content-related community reading time, book talks can introduce students to content-related print or electronic materials from the school or classroom library. As noted in Chapter 3, the purpose of a book talk is to generate enthusiasm for a book and provide a 3–5 minute book commercial. First sentences of book talks can be just as effective with informational books related to content area topics as they are with fiction. Here are some examples of books with great first sentences that promote interest:

At the age of eight, I left school and was given a job in the mines. I found it pretty hard getting out of bed at five-thirty every morning.
From *Growing Up in Coal Country* (Bartoletti, 1996)

April 24, 1990. For decades, astronomers had waited for this day. The Hubble Space Telescope, a scientific instrument that some said was one of the greatest inventions of Twentieth-Century science, lay safely tucked inside the cargo bay of space shuttle *Discovery*, waiting to be launched into orbit 370 miles above the earth.
From *Close Encounters: Exploring the Universe With the Hubble Space Telescope* (Scott, 1998)

You hear them before you see them. On a quiet day, as you approach one of the dens at the Narcisse Wildlife Management Area in Manitoba, Canada, you can hear a rustling like wind in dry leaves. It's the sound of thousands of slithering snakes.
From *The Snake Scientist* (Montgomery, 1999)

Once there was a girl who wanted to fly. She dreamed of zooming in a spaceship up through the clouds into outer space, learning new things about earth.
From *Hilary Rodham Clinton: Dreams Taking Flight* (Krull, 2008)

He is the Babe. He has always loved this game. This baseball. But what he does not know yet is this: He will change this game he loves. Forever.
From *Home Run: The Story of Babe Ruth* (Burleigh, 1998)

These examples demonstrate how good authors of informational books can grab young readers from the very beginning of the book. In the first example, the author portrays a child who works in the coal mine, creating a connection between students today and the plight of that child from the past. In the second example, the author creates enthusiasm for the Hubble telescope by showing young readers how important it was to astronomers and what questions it might answer, thereby piquing curiosity about what it was able to do.

Interactive Read-Alouds With Informational Trade Books. Reading aloud biography and informational titles related to science, social studies, mathematics, art or music, can enliven content area learning in ways that textbooks cannot. *The Librarian Who Measured the Earth* (Lasky, 1994), for example, is an excellent read-aloud book for a mathematics classroom, which describes how Eratosthenes devised a means of measuring the

Earth's circumference in the third century B.C. Describing the problem-solving processes he used as well as the underlying mathematical principles, this title represents an interesting melding of biographical and mathematical content. Biographies of this type teach students the connections between facts and faces, helping them realize that human knowledge is constructed by and through real people just like them.

All too often, classroom read-aloud experiences are isolated and unrelated to other classroom work. In classrooms where inquiry units are used, for example, read-alouds can introduce, culminate, or extend units or topics of study. During a unit on the presidency, Julie Allison read *So You Want to Be President?* (St. George, 2000) aloud to her fifth-grade class. Full of interesting and amusing anecdotes, this Caldecott Honor winner explores the characteristics of U.S. presidents present and past. It also examines the advantages and disadvantages of the presidency from a student's point of view. Advantages include having a swimming pool, a movie theater, and not having to eat broccoli, while disadvantages include having to dress up, be polite, and do lots of homework.

Pairing read-alouds from different genres can enliven content area studies. During a science unit on insects, for a third-grade class you might read aloud *Charlotte's Web* (White, 1952) and pair it with *Spiders* (Bishop, 2007), an outstanding informational title that provides sophisticated information about spiders along with full-color photographs. Students can compare the contents, the purposes of each author, and the ways each book achieved those purposes by using a Venn diagram. From these experiences, students develop understanding of the imaginative forms of fiction and the creative shaping of facts required for writing informational texts.

You can also read aloud different accounts of the same person, place, or event. For an intermediate-grade classroom, you could read aloud *Abraham Lincoln* (d'Aulaire & d'Aulaire, 2008), *Abe's Honest Words: The Life of Abraham Lincoln* (Rappaport, 2007), and *Abraham Lincoln: A Man for All the People: A Ballad* (Livingston, 1993). In this way, students can examine different authors' points of view about this extraordinary man's life. The first title, which was originally published in 1939, presents an idealized version of Lincoln's life. It avoids mention of the assassination, since this fact was considered too harsh for inclusion in a children's book of that time. The second book uses Lincoln's words and extraordinary illustrations to depict his life. The third work uses a narrative poem to lyrically recount the events that shaped Lincoln's life. Following these readings, students could compare the form of each book, the points of view each author took toward its subject, and the information each chose to include or exclude.

Most books mentioned so far in this section are best read in their entirety. Many informational titles, however, are not appropriate for cover-to-cover reading. For this reason, you may want to read aloud bits and pieces of books to whet students' appetites for information.

Reading picture captions is one form of bits-and-pieces reading aloud that can provide a sneak preview of a book. The lengthy captions for the pictures and documents in *Anne Frank: Beyond the Diary* (van der Rol & Verhoeven, 1993) for example, connect artifacts to the diary itself. Beneath a photo of Otto Frank glued inside Anne's diary, the author explains that Anne was particularly attached to her father, who provided her with love and support during the long days of hiding from the Nazis. Brief vignettes from books like Krull's (2002) *Lives of the Musicians: Good Times, Bad Times, (and What the Neighbors Thought)* make great 5–10 minute read-alouds. You could read one of Krull's brief, amusing vignettes about Mozart, Beethoven, or other musicians at the beginning of class.

Reading content area trade books aloud helps you to capitalize on students' natural curiosity about a wide range of topics. It can heighten student interest in the world around them and provide an opportunity for in-depth exploration of curricular topics that textbooks cannot. In addition, it builds familiarity with this genre by exposing students to the language and organizational patterns of expository text. Table 16 provides a list of great content-related read-alouds for science, social studies, art, and music.

SIRT in the Content Area Classroom

Depending upon the model you select, SIRT in the content area classroom might occur daily for a specified time or just once a week. Regardless of the model chosen, you want to include any or all of the following activities: focus lessons, time for reading, student–teacher conferences, and response to reading. As is true in the language arts classroom, a typical schedule for SIRT in the content area classroom would involve 15 minutes of large-group focus lessons, 30 minutes for individual reading, and 15 minutes for students to complete response to reading. Embedded within this time are student–teacher conferences of about 5–15 minutes.

Table 16. Great Books for Content Area Read-Alouds

Content Area	Primary Grades (K–2)	Intermediate Grades (3–4)	Upper Grades (5–6)	All Ages
Mathematics	• *The Greedy Triangle* (Burns, 2008)	• *The Man Who Made Time Travel* (Lasky, 2003) • *Math Talk: Mathematical Ideas in Poems for Two Voices* (Pappas, 1991) • *Sir Cumference and the New Round Table: A Math Adventure* (Neuschwander, 1999)	• *G Is for Googol: A Math Alphabet Book* (Schwartz, 1998)	• *Math Curse* (Scieszka, 1995)
Social studies	• *Abe's Honest Words: The Life of Abraham Lincoln* (Rappaport, 2007) • *Building Manhattan* (Vila, 2008)	• *Save Queen of Sheba* (Moeri, 1994)	• *Bodies From the Ash: Life and Death in Ancient Pompeii* (Deem, 2005) • *Maritcha: A Nineteenth Century American Girl* (Bolden, 2005)	• *Through My Eyes* (Bridges, 1999)
Science	• *An Egg Is Quiet* (Aston & Long, 2006) • *Spectacular Science: A Book of Poems* (Hopkins, 2002)	• *To Space and Back* (Ride & Okie, 1986)	• *Life on Earth: The Story of Evolution* (Jenkins, 2002)	
Art	• *Action Jackson* (Greenberg & Jordan, 2002) • *Diego* (Winter, 2007) • *Vincent's Colors* (van Gogh, 2005)	• *The Yellow House: Vincent van Gogh and Paul Gauguin Side by Side* (Rubin, 2001)	• *Leonardo: Beautiful Dreamer* (Byrd, 2003)	
Music	• *John Coltrane's Giant Steps* (Raschka, 2002) • *When Marian Sang: The True Recital of Marian Anderson: The Voice of a Century* (Ryan, 2001)	• *The Philharmonic Gets Dressed* (Kuskin, 2008)	• *I See the Rhythm* (Igus, 1998)	• *Jazz* (Myers, 2006)

Focus Lessons

As noted previously, short, focused lessons provide instruction in the skills that students need to read independently. In Chapter 3, we discussed the kinds of focus lessons you need to address, many of which are certainly appropriate for the content area independent reading program. Here we offer additional content-related focus lessons designed to help students (a) read a range of texts associated with specific content area subjects, (b) understand the types of visuals they may encounter within that text type, (c) comprehend text structures and formats, and (d) write in the discourse forms found in the content area. Regardless of the type of lesson, you need to model what students are to do, give guided practice that supports them as they try out the strategy or procedure, and give opportunities for independent practice in performing the desired behavior. Chapter 4 provides additional information on this approach. The following sections describe examples of the types of focus lessons you should address, and Table 17 offers examples of focus lesson activities in each of these categories for both social studies and science.

Table 17. Focus Lesson Activities for Independent Reading in Social Studies and Science

Focus Area	Social Studies	Science
Reading text types	• Reading primary source texts • Analyzing primary source photographs • Reading newspaper articles	• Reading experiments • Reading scientific reports • Reading field guides
Reading visual texts	• Identifying text features • Reading maps • Reading timelines • Reading data charts	• Identifying text features • Reading flowcharts • Reading life-cycle visuals • Reading time-lapse photographs
Reading text structures	• Reading cause–effect structures • Reading descriptive structures	• Reading steps in a process • Reading problem–solution structures
Understanding academic language	• Teaching content-related root words, prefixes, and suffixes	• Teaching content-related root words, prefixes, and suffixes
Writing texts	• Writing historical accounts • Writing compare–contrast essays	• Writing observational records • Writing laboratory reports

Familiarizing With Different Text Types. You must provide explicit instruction in reading a range of texts, including diaries, maps, memoirs, journals, and photographs. Helping students to consider the historical context of the document, the biases and viewpoints of the author, and the unique language of the document are essential if students are to realize the importance of primary sources. For example, students who are doing independent reading in social studies may encounter newspaper articles, either on the Internet or reproduced in trade books. Teaching students the inverted pyramid style of a newspaper article can facilitate comprehension by helping them look for the answers to who, what, when, where, and why questions in the first few paragraphs of the article. Teaching students how to read various text types in the science classroom, including experiments, field journals, and other forms, is equally important.

Making Meaning From Visual Texts. Today's content area trade books are replete with stunning visuals, but we cannot assume that students understand them. Instructing students in understanding flowcharts, life-cycle diagrams, and other forms of visual text in science, for example, helps develop readers and writers in academic disciplines.

Reading Common Text Structures. The ability to recognize structures like description, sequence, compare and contrast, cause and effect, and problem and solution are essential for reading and understanding content-related materials. For example, when reading the directions for completion of an experiment, students need to understand that the steps in a process are typically arranged sequentially. Teaching students about the signal words that accompany this structure, such as *first, second, next*, and *then* can enhance comprehension.

Learning Academic Vocabulary. Teaching students about academic vocabulary, particularly through root words, prefixes, and suffixes, can facilitate independent understanding of many content related terms.

Writing in Discourse Forms. Involving students in writing in the genre they encounter in particular content areas can develop deep understanding of specific discourse forms. Writing newspaper articles and compare–contrast essays in social studies or laboratory reports and field journals in science can engage students and promote facility with the linguistic forms of the content area.

Sample Focus Lesson: Analyzing Historical Documents

Many children's books contain original documents that can provide the basis for studying the past. Hopkinson's (2004) *Shutting Out the Sky: Life in the Tenements of New York, 1880–1924* is replete with interesting photographs of families living in New York tenements between 1880 and 1924. The frontispiece, for example, contains a photograph of a family seated in their apartment.

During a focus lesson with upper-grade students, you could introduce a sequence for studying photographs that allows students to "read" pictures and develop visual literacy skills whereby they collect data and draw inferences about a visual text. To do this, students can follow a specific sequence for analyzing historical photographs (Barton, 2001; Felton & Allen, 1990; see Table 18).

Table 18. Analyzing Historical Photographs

Steps	Application
Make predictions	Engage students in predicting what might be in the photograph. Record their predictions.
Introduce the photograph	Present the photograph, providing students with some background information on it.
Reflect on the photograph	Have students move their eyes clockwise around the photograph, recording notes about what they see.
Ask questions	Help students draw inferences based upon their observations and provide opportunities for them to modify, abandon, or confirm earlier predictions.
Evaluate predictions	Check predictions against information provided in a variety of additional sources such as textbooks or the Internet.
Review the process	Review the process with students and focus their attention on each of the different stages. Ask students to reflect on what they have learned from their analysis of the photograph.

Note. Adapted from Barton, K.C. (2001). A picture's worth: Analyzing historical photographs in the elementary grades. *Social Education, 65*(5), 278–283; Felton, R.G., & Allen, R.F. (1990). Using visual materials as historical sources: A model for studying state and local history. *The Social Studies, 81*(2), 84–87.

For example, during the first step of the process—prediction—encourage students to predict and record their predictions about what they might see in a photograph of a family living in a tenement. Following this, give students copies of the photograph and ask them to record notes about what they see in the photograph. They can identify or label people, groups, or objects in the photograph and share these observations with a partner.

During the next step in the process, introduce the photograph and ask students to reflect on what they see, and then ask them questions designed to help them make inferences about the photograph. For example, during an analysis of the photograph described earlier, you could ask, What can you tell about the people in the photograph from the way they are dressed? Where do you think they are living? What can you tell about their living conditions from this photograph? Have students draw inferences about this information, potentially by consulting online resources or even the text itself to see what else they might learn about the family in the photograph.

Following this lesson, students can read and examine books with photographs during their time for reading and later share their perceptions during their conference or with a small group of peers. Finally, students can review the thinking process in which they have engaged. These steps can easily be applied to photographs found in books such as *A Dream of Freedom: The Civil Rights Movement From 1954–1968* (McWhorter, 2005) and many other nonfiction books.

Time for Reading

As noted in Chapter 3, during the 30-minute reading block students (a) practice reading in an appropriate book and apply what they have learned during the focus lessons and (b) participate with you in a conference. If at all possible, students should read silently, or if they are younger, in pairs. With these younger students, you might want to break up reading time into two parts: 15 minutes for silent or whisper reading and 15 minutes for paired reading.

During time for reading, you might elect to give students book choices within certain limits rather than free choice. For example, if you are focusing on helping students analyze primary-source photographs, provide students with a set of preselected books or bookmark websites that contain these materials.

Student–Teacher Conferences

Teacher-led conferences help monitor student progress toward a variety of content-related literacy goals, both general and specific, during content area independent reading. Use these conference times to assess students' progress in terms of their motivation in relation to a content area, attitude toward reading that type of content, ability to select and engage with texts, and use of reading strategies, oral fluency, and text comprehension. During this time you might interview students, conduct running records, review student written responses to texts, and so on. There might be additional times during the day when you can conduct reading conferences outside of the 30-minute block of reading time.

Conferences allow you to differentiate instruction to the needs of the student and focus on many aspects of content area literacy including broad literacy goals such as student motivation for reading in a content area or narrower skills like academic vocabulary. Some areas might be easily addressed in one or two conferences, while others might require attention over a period of months. In the sections that follow, we provide examples of two types of conferences: book-selection conferences and book-focused conferences.

Book-Selection Conferences. You may wish to conduct a reading conference designed to help students select books in a particular content area early in the school year. Prior to conducting the individual conferences, you should consult students' reading logs (see Chapter 3) and review any information about the students' reading levels, especially as related to informational texts.

During this conference, ask students to answer a variety of questions related to reading motivation in a particular content area. The Recording Form for Content Reading Motivation Conference for Science (see Appendix A) provides sample questions for assessing reading motivation in science. You can ask these questions or others appropriate to a content area and record student responses. Then present the student with three or four content area books appropriate to his or her reading level and interest. Review with the student how to select a book of appropriate difficulty and note which books were most interesting to the student.

Book Focused Conferences. Some conferences focus on the extent to which students are experiencing success in reading content-related independent reading books. Check for student understanding through running records, retellings, or comprehension questions appropriate to the book. There are many different questions you can ask students about content-related books during conferences. Table 19 provides a list of potential questions for an informational text comprehension conference. In Chapter 3, we provided an example of a conference for a fiction book; here we detail a conference for an informational book with a second grader named Andrea. As part of this conference, the teacher chose to have Andrea answer some questions and complete a retelling to demonstrate her comprehension of the text. She then recorded Andrea's responses on the Content Reading Conference Record (see Appendix A).

"Andrea, please show me your reading folder and the book you have been reading. I see that you have completed one book during the past week," the teacher begins. "You selected the book *Sarah Morton's Day: A Day in the Life of a Pilgrim Girl* [Waters & Kendall, 2008]. Today I would like to ask you some questions about the book and then have you do a retelling. Can you tell me a little bit about Sarah Morton and where she lived?"

"Yes, Sarah Morton was a little girl who lived in Pilgrim times in a village."

"Now I'd like for you to tell me everything you can remember about the book. You can take a few minutes to look over the pictures before you start. Try to remember as much as you can in the same order as the story was told in the book."

Andrea provides the following retelling of the book:
"On the first page, she introduces herself and tells about the village she lives in. She gets up and puts her clothes on and rolls up her bed. Then she has to start the fire and help her mom make the pudding like oatmeal. She has to stand up to eat, but her mom and stepdad get to sit down. Her stepfather will soon make her a stool so that she can sit down. Then she has to feed the roosters. Then she has to milk the cows, and she calls for her friend Elizabeth. She and Elizabeth tell stories and secrets to each other. After milking the cow she has to muck the garden for rich planting in the spring. Then her and her mom make butter. And then her mother and her make Indian corn bread, and when her stepfather gets home they eat supper. After dinner she has to polish the brass which is their dishes. Then they say they see a ship coming in. Her mom says she can get Elizabeth to see it, but it's only a tiny little speck. When she comes back her stepdad thinks she shows a talent for learning. He makes her learn her ABCs and reading. Then she has to go milk the goats. After that he says he likes having a daughter. Her

Table 19. Sample Questions for Content Area Reading Conference

Type of Question	Sample Questions
Response questions	• Why did you pick this book? • Did the book meet your expectations? Why or why not? • Would you tell a friend to read this book? Why or why not?
Content questions	• What was the topic of your book? • What are the main ideas in this book? • How was the information organized? • Were there any interesting visuals in the book, such as maps, graphs, charts, and so on? • Would you like to read more about this topic? Why or why not? • What is the most interesting thing you learned from the book?

mother calls for her and they set off for the spring for the next day's water. They talk about her new father and if she likes him and how they're getting along. Then she tells her mother and father good night, gets her bedding ready, takes off her clothes, and tells her poppet the day's events. Then she says her prayers and that's it."

"That was a great retelling, Andrea. You really remembered lots of details and told the story in the exact order it happened in the book. What was your favorite part of the book?" the teacher asks.

"My favorite part was when she was with her friend Elizabeth that she told secrets to."

"Good. Can you think of some ways her life was different from yours?"

"She lived long ago. She had to help her mom a lot and milk the cows."

"Did you like this book?"

"It was pretty good," says Andrea.

"Did it help you understand what we are studying in social studies?"

"Yes. I liked seeing how she dressed. I liked the photographs."

At this point, the teacher prompts Andrea to identify other connections between this book and social studies learning. In addition, she suggests other books for Andrea based on her interests.

Response to Reading Activities

Responses to content-related books can involve completion of graphic organizers, dramatic activities, inquiry activities, and written responses. Chapter 4 contains a variety of suggestions for response activities appropriate to many texts. Here we focus on one type of response activity that we have found to be especially useful in the content classroom: idea circles.

Idea circles are a form of response that is uniquely suited to content area independent reading because they allow students to engage in small-group, peer-led discussions of concepts fueled by reading experiences with multiple texts (Guthrie & McCann, 1996). Idea circles are an ideal way to promote peer-directed conceptual understanding of virtually any aspect of content area learning. This conceptual learning involves three basic ingredients: facts, relationships between facts, and explanations. Idea circles require that students locate information, evaluate its quality and relevance, summarize information for their peers, and determine relationships among information found in a variety of sources. They require that students learn to integrate information, ideas, and viewpoints. In addition, they involve students in group processes, including turn taking, maintaining group member participation, and coaching one another in the use of literacy strategies (Guthrie & McCann, 1996).

Idea circles share some common elements with literature circles. Like literature circles, idea circles involve three to six students in directed small-group discussions. Like literature circles, idea circles are peer led and involve student-generated rules, but idea circles involve students in discussion surrounding the learning of a particular concept rather than an entire text. In literature circle discussions, students may have conflicting interpretations of a piece of literature. With idea circles, students work together to create a common understanding of a concept by constructing abstract understanding from facts and details.

Idea circles are especially applicable to independent reading because every student reads a different text in preparation for the group discussion. During the discussion, students share the unique information that they have found. Furthermore, idea circle discussions require the use of informational, rather than literary, texts. When used as part of a unit of study, idea circles are most effective when placed at the middle or end of a unit.

Begin the idea circle experience by presenting students with a goal in the form of a topic or question. An example question might be, How might global warming affect future generations of people around the world? Before the idea circle meets, students should read extensively from relevant informational trade books to gather information on the topic.

They may also bring information to the group from prior experiences or discussions with others. In their groups, students exchange facts, discuss relationships among ideas, and offer explanations. As facts are woven together, students create a conceptual framework around the topic or question. Individuals offer information, corroborate it with others, and discuss more deeply. Students should continually challenge one another regarding the accuracy and relevance of their information. Through this checking, they are encouraged to search for information, comprehend the texts being used, and synthesize information from multiple sources. When conflicts arise, students search their sources to clarify conflicting information. Ultimately, the group must weave together the important details that all students contribute.

To get started with idea circles in your classroom, you can follow these six simple steps:

1. Decide whether to engage the entire class in idea circles simultaneously or start with a single team and gradually add more.

2. Identify appropriate topics of study. It should be interesting and expansive and promote a critical stance toward reading.

3. Set clear goals about what each group should accomplish during their discussions. Students may complete data charts, semantic maps, or other graphic organizers.

4. Provide students with trade books and other resources at a variety of levels related to the topic under study.

5. Students must read and learn about the topic before participating in the idea circle, and they should refine their understanding as they continue to read during the experience.

6. Ask students to develop rules for group interaction (Vacca & Vacca, 2008).

During a social studies study on the U.S. Civil War, teacher Anna Muñoz involved her students in using idea circles to promote inquiry. She divided students into three groups, and each was assigned to study a different population involved with the war: slaves, planters, and soldiers. Ms. Muñoz focused student inquiry through questions like these: What did the Civil War mean to each of these groups? How was each group affected by the war? What were their viewpoints and attitudes about the war? Students consulted a variety of sources, including trade books, textbooks, and websites, to locate answers to these questions. Finally, the students were reconfigured into new, smaller groups so that each contained a member from the previous three groups. The final product for the idea circle was for each small group to complete a data chart comparing and contrasting each of the three different Civil War populations.

Assessment and Record Keeping

During SIRT, students are responsible for maintaining records that they keep in their reading folders and bring to their reading conferences. All of these are detailed in Chapter 3, and include the following items:

- Reading Interest Forms
- Reading Logs
- Response to reading materials
- Self-evaluation rubrics

Students maintain records of reading topics of interest and book titles they would like to read on the Reading Interest Forms (see Appendix A). Students can maintain records of the books they are reading on their Reading Logs (see Appendix A) as well as their evaluation of the books. In addition, students maintain copies of responses to reading in their folders. They should also maintain records of their own progress by using the Independent Reading Self-Evaluation Rubric (see Appendix A).

Your own record keeping should involve completion of the forms described in Chapter 3, including the weekly Independent Reading Observation Rubric for Teachers. In addition, record notes from conferences on the Content Reading Conference Record described earlier in this chapter (also see Appendix A). This form provides space for completing running records as well as student responses to comprehension questions. As with the evaluation rubrics, comparison of these forms over time can demonstrate student growth in terms of both fluency and comprehension. Furthermore, you can compare your scores with students' and discuss areas of discrepancy.

Creating a content area independent reading program lets you promote content area learning through myriad texts, not just textbooks. By setting aside time for reading in the content area classroom, you expose students to information while you help them develop funds of knowledge about subjects that matter both in and out of school. Appendix B contains a reproducible tip sheet you can give to parents, too, to encourage students' independent content area reading at home. Through independent content area reading, students develop the literacy skills they need to succeed in the world of the 21st century.

A DISCUSSION WITH MYRA ZARNOWSKI

Myra Zarnowski is a professor in the Department of Elementary and Early Childhood Education at Queens College, City University of New York, where she teaches courses in literacy, children's literature, and social studies. A former classroom teacher, she has taught at both the elementary and middle school levels. She is particularly interested in making history a vibrant subject for teachers and students. Zarnowski's most recent books are *History Makers: A Questioning Approach to Reading and Writing Biographies* and *Making Sense of History: Using High-Quality Literature and Hands-On Experiences to Build Content Knowledge.*

Terrell Young: Recently social studies have been pushed out of the curriculum. Why is instruction in social studies so important?

Myra Zarnowski: There have been many articles and reports about social studies being put "on the back burner." Mostly, this is because there isn't enough time to schedule it in if math and reading are to be given the lion's share of the school day. There is some contradictory evidence, though, that teachers are learning to integrate social studies lessons into to the language arts block. While that is promising, it isn't really enough.

Why? Social studies teaching focuses on unique goals. The most important goal is preparing students to be active and informed citizens who are skilled decision makers. To make good decisions, students need information. But information shouldn't be swallowed whole. Instead, it needs to be examined critically the way historians and social scientists do. Social studies involves teaching students how to learn information about the past and the present, to critically evaluate this information, and then to do something active with it. This kind of learning is crucial to preparing citizens in a democracy and certainly too important to be put on the back burner.

TY: Why do you so strongly advocate for the use of trade books in content area study?

MZ: The most important reason to use trade books is that they are good to think with. Researchers have pointed out many times that trade books are better written than textbooks. They've been called "considerate" because they take into account that young readers need background information to make sense of the past. Trade books also are more comprehensible because they are more clearly written, more descriptive, and more anecdotal. They develop ideas in more detail than textbooks. All of this makes them more interesting to read. Readers like them!

In addition, trade books in history often contain authors' notes telling readers things like how the author became interested in the topic, where he or she found the information in the book, and what information is still unknown. This helps readers understand that the past is still a topic for exciting inquiry.

I could go on and on about this, but I'll end with one idea: Trade books are written by people who are authentically interested in social studies topics. This enthusiasm is contagious. It's even been called *viral*. If children, too, become interested in social studies topics, they will be motivated to pursue them.

TY: What do you see as the role of independent reading in content area learning?

MZ: Independent reading is essential. Reading history is a specialized kind of reading. It involves paying attention to such things as the historical context, multiple perspectives, the significance of information, and the reliability of sources. It involves carefully examining documents and photographs. This takes practice. Teachers can model how to do this, but students need time to practice by themselves. Independent reading provides a chance for them to get this practice.

Independent reading also introduces readers to exemplary authors such as Russell Freedman, Diane Stanley, Jim Murphy, Tonya Bolden, Candace Fleming, Deborah Hopkinson, Martin Sandler, James Cross Giblin, and so many more. Reading books by these authors not only opens up the world of historical nonfiction for children, but also introduces excellent models for student writing.

TY: What are your greatest concerns with the classroom libraries you see when you walk into classrooms?

MZ: I am concerned that there are not enough quality nonfiction books. It's easy to identify recommended books in social studies. Each year, the National Council for the Social Studies puts out a list of Notable Social Studies Tradebooks for Young People. These lists are available on the Internet. Other excellent lists for social studies teachers include the Orbis Pictus Award for

Outstanding Nonfiction for Children and the Sibert Medal. Unfortunately, I do not often see these books in classroom libraries. When I do see them, they are not displayed prominently. Students might not select them because they are on unfamiliar topics. Social studies books need to be book talked by the teacher. Then students need to have enough time to read them. I am especially concerned about that.

TY: What is the best advice you have for teachers regarding the implementation and monitoring of independent reading in the content areas?

MZ: Share your enthusiasm for reading social studies books. Provide information about how to read critically and model the process. Provide time for children to share their responses to literature with their classmates and with you. Keep notes on each child's reading, and spend time conferencing with individual students. Have students keep logs about their independent reading, noting the books they are reading and their responses to these books. Consider how to help students use outstanding trade books as models for their writing. Read new books and share intriguing parts with your students. Have students recommend books to each other.

TY: After the National Reading Panel report, many people have suggested that independent reading should take place outside of school. What is your response to that suggestion?

MZ: I think independent reading should be part of the school day. This is when children are usually alert and ready to learn. And because independent reading is a major source of learning, it is an appropriate school activity. Students in the elementary school build their stamina for independent reading over time. An observant teacher knows when to end the reading time. This teacher is also available to make suggestions for student reading—which book would be a great follow-up or would be something new to try. Finally, a teacher is there to answer questions and see where student comprehension is breaking down and instruction is needed to remedy this.

It is, of course, wonderful if—in addition—students also read at home. But I think we should acknowledge that independent reading is not a frill or a time for goofing off. It's the way children develop the habit of reading and grow into lifelong readers.

TY: What do you view as the role of instruction during independent reading time?

MZ: I think the main activity during independent reading should be reading. However, there are times when teachers can pull aside students to recommend books or answer questions about material in books. Sometimes students are confused by a word, phrase, or illustration in a book. Teachers can intervene to get the students back on track. Overall, I think undisturbed reading is what should be taking place.

Reproducibles for the Classroom

Reading Interest Form
Reading Log
Reading Conference Record
Independent Reading Self-Evaluation Rubric
Independent Reading Observation Rubric for Teachers
Inferring From Text Graphic Organizer
Recording Form for Content Reading Motivation
    Conference for Science
Content Reading Conference Record

READING INTEREST FORM

Topics I Am Interested In	Books I Want to Read

READING LOG

Title of the Book	My Rating of the Book ✓✓✓✓ Excellent book ✓✓✓ Good book ✓✓ Book was OK ✓ Did not like the book	Why I Liked or Did Not Like the Book

READING CONFERENCE RECORD

Student name _____

Conference date _____

Title of book student is reading _____

Goal for pages read by next conference _____

Focus of conference _____

Running record:

Comprehension questions: (Select questions from the list provided in Table 13 and record here)

1.

Student response:

2.

Student response:

3.

Student response:

4.

Student response:

5.

Student response:

INDEPENDENT READING
SELF-EVALUATION RUBRIC

Independent Reading Self-Evaluation for Week of _____				
Reading Areas	1 Below Expectations	2 Approaching Expectations	3 Meets Expectations	4 Exceeds Expectations
Selects books of appropriate interest and difficulty				
Student comments:				
Sets and meets appropriate reading goals				
Student comments:				
Reads a variety of genres				
Student comments:				
Demonstrates motivation for reading				
Student comments:				
Demonstrates strategies for identifying new words				
Student comments:				
Reads with fluency and expression				
Student comments:				
Comprehends fictional texts				
Student comments:				
Comprehends informational texts				
Student comments:				
Target skill for week				
Teacher comments:				

INDEPENDENT READING OBSERVATION RUBRIC FOR TEACHERS

Independent Reading Observation Rubric for (student name) _____
Week of _____

Reading Areas	1 Below Expectations	2 Approaching Expectations	3 Meets Expectations	4 Exceeds Expectations
Selects books of appropriate interest and difficulty				
Teacher comments:				
Sets and meets appropriate reading goals				
Teacher comments:				
Reads a variety of genres				
Teacher comments:				
Demonstrates motivation for reading				
Teacher comments:				
Demonstrates strategies for identifying new words				
Teacher comments:				
Reads with fluency and expression				
Teacher comments:				
Comprehends fictional texts				
Teacher comments:				
Comprehends informational texts				
Teacher comments:				
Sets appropriate reading goals				
Teacher comments:				
Target skill for week				
Teacher comments:				

INFERRING FROM TEXT GRAPHIC ORGANIZER

Text _____

_____

_____

_____

I wonder _____

_____

Maybe _____

Text _____

_____

_____

_____

I wonder _____

_____

Maybe _____

Text _____

_____

_____

_____

I wonder _____

_____

Maybe _____

Text _____

_____

_____

_____

I wonder _____

_____

Maybe _____

I'm inferring that _____

_____

_____

_____

_____

_____

_____

Developed by Nicole Blake

RECORDING FORM FOR CONTENT READING MOTIVATION CONFERENCE FOR SCIENCE

1. Do you enjoy science? Why or why not?

2. Do you think of yourself as a scientist? Why or why not?

3. What kinds of science do you most enjoy?

4. Can you remember any science activities you have done in school that you really liked?

5. Can you think of a science book that you enjoyed reading? What was it about?

Here are some topics that you might find in science class. Which ones would be most interesting to you?

Dinosaurs	Famous scientists	The ocean	Space
The earth	Food and nutrition	Pets	Technology
Energy	Insects	Plants	Weather
The environment	Jungle animals	Rocks and minerals	

Observation Notes:

Book Selection Strategies Observed:

Book Preferences Notes:

Adapted from Hill, B.C., & Ruptic, C. (1994). *Practical aspects of authentic assessment: Putting the pieces together.* Norwood, MA: Christopher Gordon.

CONTENT READING CONFERENCE RECORD

Student name _____

Conference date _____

Title of book student is reading _____

Goals for pages read by next meeting _____

Focus of conference _____

Comprehension questions (select questions provided in Table 19 and record here)

1.

Student response:

2.

Student response:

3.

Student response:

4.

Student response:

5.

Student response:

(continued)

CONTENT READING CONFERENCE RECORD *(cont.)*

Retelling

Directions

> Now I would like for you to tell me everything you can remember about the book. You can take a few minutes to look over the pictures before you start. Try to remember as much as you can in the same order as the story was told in the book.

Record retelling here

Retelling Rating

___Excellent   ___Fair   ___Poor

Notes:

Follow-Up Questions:

Teacher Comments:

Reproducible Handouts for Parents

Creating Your Home Library
Helping Your Child Pick Good Books
Promoting Interest in Content Area Reading at Home

Creating Your Home Library

Every family should have a home library; it demonstrates to children of all ages that books matter enough to have an honored place in the home. A home library can help you encourage your child to choose reading and to discover the joys and pleasure of reading from an early age. A home library can build a strong foundation for reading, which has lifelong benefits for your child both in and out of school.

A home library requires two things: space and reading materials. The following pointers can help you create a home library that you and your child will enjoy.

Creating the Space

- Find a space for the library. It can be in your child's bedroom, in a small corner of your living room, or in another small area.

- Create a book storage area. Books can be stored on bookshelves, on brick and board shelves, in baskets, or on plastic crates or stacking cubes.

- Create a place for your child to sit and read if you have room. Child-size chairs or beanbag chairs and a good lamp can create a cozy space for reading.

Stocking the Collection

- Help your child select books or other reading materials for the collection. Books can be purchased inexpensively through school book clubs or book fairs, through local library or yard sales, and online at sites like Book Closeout (www.bookcloseouts.com). For younger children, provide sturdy board books.

- Virtually any kind of reading material can become part of the home library. Newspapers, magazines, song books, catalogs, pamphlets, and almanacs are just a few of the kinds of print materials that children can enjoy.

- Give books or magazine subscriptions as birthday and holiday gifts.

(continued)

- Understand that the quality of the collection is more important than the quantity. Include books that children love and will read over and over. Provide books at a variety of reading levels.

- Involve your child in creating their own books that can be added to the collection. Your child can write and illustrate his or her own stories in blank books that can be purchased inexpensively, or on construction paper that you bind with staples, tape, or string.

- Have your child demonstrate pride in his or her books by creating decorative bookplates for their books. On the bookplate he or she can write "From the library of _____." These can then be glued into the front cover of each book. Or your child can decorate the inside cover or title page with his or her name.

Displaying the Collection

- Display books with covers facing out. Group books together by your child's favorite topics. Put books for younger children on the lowest shelves.

- Display favorite objects next to books if there is room. For example, you might place seashells collected at the beach next to a book on oceans.

- Assist your child in alphabetizing books by author or arranging books by genres. This helps organize the collection and provides practice in important skills.

Helping Your Child Pick Good Books

- Take your child to the library frequently.

- Give your child books for birthdays and holidays. Store these books in a special place.

- Know your child's interests and where books related to those interests can be found.

- Pay attention to the books your child loves. Look for another book by the same author or on the same topic.

- Use online resources for parents like Reading Rockets (www .readingrockets.org) or RIF (www.rif.org) to find lists of books for children and pointers for parents.

- Teach your child the five-finger test for finding books that aren't too difficult. With this technique, children select a page in a prospective book choice and count, using their fingers on one hand, the number of unknown words found on the page. If there are five or more words, the book may be too difficult.

- Share your own reading with your child.

- Create a positive vibe around books and reading through your attitude:

  "I found you a great book about Babe Ruth because I know you love baseball. Let's read it together."

  "Let's talk about the book you are reading. Why do you think the author wrote the book?"

  "You can stay up an hour later tonight, as long as you are reading."

  "For your birthday I got you *Ranger Rick* magazine. I think you will love reading the articles in it. Can you find one and read it to me while I make dinner?"

Promoting Interest in Content Area Reading at Home

Teachers are responsible for promoting independent reading at school. But you can do a lot to encourage content area independent reading in the classroom and at home, too. Encouraging your child to read informational books at home helps your child do better in school subjects like social studies and science. Here are some suggestions:

- Make books part of the environment. Find opportunities to connect books to your child's life. Place books about fish near the aquarium or books about hamsters near the hamster cage or children's books about cooking in the kitchen.

- Take your child to libraries, museums, and parks. Community-based learning experiences provide a natural springboard to learning and can easily be connected with books. If you take your child to see dinosaur bones at the Museum of Natural History, for instance, find a book about dinosaurs you can read together. If your family visits Sea World, find books about dolphins or whales that would interest your child.

- Read about famous people. Many children enjoy biographies about their favorite sports personalities, actors, musicians, or authors. Keeping a supply of interesting biographies available can heighten engagement and help students identify with their heroes. Reading about famous people in magazines like *Sports Illustrated Kids* or *Time for Kids* can motivate children to read more.

- Read to complete a task. Many children enjoy creating things, whether preparing a meal, making a friendship bracelet, or creating a family scrapbook. Give your child a book or manual to read to complete a task— this builds skill in following directions and makes reading interesting.

- Read about hobbies. Hobbies are a natural entrance into the world of reading. Books and magazines about skateboarding, basketball, dancing, art, or music let children explore the things that interest them and provide reading opportunities that may not be available at school.

REFERENCES

Adams, M.J. (1990). *Beginning to read: Thinking and learning about print*. Cambridge, MA: MIT Press.

Adomat, D.S. (2009). Actively engaging with stories through drama: Portraits of two young readers. *The Reading Teacher, 62*(8), 628–636. doi:10.1598/RT.62.8.1

Allington, R.L. (1994). The schools we have. The schools we need. *The Reading Teacher, 48*(1), 14–29.

Allington, R.L. (2006). *What really matters for struggling readers: Designing research-based programs* (2nd ed.). Boston: Allyn & Bacon.

Allington, R.L. (2009a). If they don't read much...30 years later. In E.H. Hiebert, (Ed.), *Reading more, reading better* (pp. 30–54). New York: Guilford.

Allington, R.L. (2009b). *What really matters in response to intervention: Research-based designs*. Boston: Allyn & Bacon/Pearson.

Allington, R.L., & McGill-Franzen, A. (2003). The impact of summer setback on the reading achievement gap. *Phi Delta Kappan, 85*(1), 68–75.

Allington, R.L., McGill-Franzen, A., Williams, L., Zmach, C., Love-Zeig, J., & Graff, J. (2007, April). *Ameliorating summer reading loss among economically disadvantaged children*. Paper presented at the American Educational Research Association Conference, Chicago, IL.

Anderson, R.C., Wilson, P.T., & Fielding, L.G. (1988). Growth in reading and how children spend their time outside of school. *Reading Research Quarterly, 23*(3), 285–303. doi:10.1598/RRQ.23.3.2

Applebee, A.N., Langer, J.A., Nystrand, M., & Gamoran, A. (2003). Discussion-based approaches to developing understanding: Classroom instruction and student performance in middle and high school English. *American Educational Research Journal, 40*(2), 685–730.

Applegate, A.J., & Applegate, M.D. (2004). The Peter effect: Reading habits and attitudes of preservice teachers. *The Reading Teacher, 57*(6), 554–563.

Artley, A.S. (1975). Good teachers of reading—Who are they? *The Reading Teacher, 29*(1), 26–31.

Asher, S.R., & Markell, R.A. (1974). Sex differences in comprehension of high- and low-interest reading material. *Journal of Educational Psychology, 66*(5), 614–619. doi: 10 .1037/h0037483

Asselin, M. (2003). Bridging the gap between learning to be male and learning to read. *Teacher Librarian, 30*(3), 53–54.

Association for Library Service to Children. (1996). *The library-museum-Head Start partnership: A national project with local impact. 1992–1996*. Chicago: American Library Association.

Barrentine, S.J. (1996). Engaging with reading through interactive read-alouds. *The Reading Teacher, 50*(1), 36–43.

Barton, K.C. (2001). A picture's worth: Analyzing historical photographs in the elementary grades. *Social Education, 65*(5), 278–283.

Baumann, J.F., Hoffman, J.V., Duffy-Hester, A.M., & Ro, J.M. (2000). The First R yesterday and today: U.S. elementary reading instruction practices reported by teachers and administrators. *Reading Research Quarterly, 35*(3), 338–377. doi:10 .1598/RRQ.35.3.2

Bernhardt, E.B. (2000). Second-language reading as a case study of reading scholarship in the 20th century. In M.L. Kamil, P.B. Mosenthal, P.D. Pearson, & R. Barr (Eds.), *Handbook of reading research* (Vol. 3, pp. 791–811). Mahwah, NJ: Erlbaum.

Biancarosa, G., & Snow, C.E. (2004). *Reading next: A vision for action and research in middle and high school literacy: A report to the Carnegie Corporation of New York.* Washington, DC: Alliance for Excellent Education.

Bishop, R.S. (1990). Mirrors, windows, and sliding glass doors. In H. Moir, M. Cain, & L. Prosak-Beres (Eds.), *Collected perspectives: Choosing and using books for the classroom* (pp. ix–xi). Boston: Christopher-Gordon.

Blachowicz, C.L.Z., & Fisher, P.J. (2009). *Teaching vocabulary in all classrooms* (4th ed.). Boston: Allyn & Bacon/Merrill Education.

Blatt, G.T. (1981). *The functions of reading in four elementary classrooms and their effects on children's reading interests.* (ERIC Document Reproduction Service ED No. 214103.

Block, C.C., Cleveland, M.D., & Reed, K.M. (2005). Using books to raise student achievement: 2nd, 3rd, 4th, and 6th grade study 2003–2004. Retrieved January 20, 2010, from teacher.scholastic.com/products/research/pdfs/ER_Using_books.pdf.

Block, C.C., & Mangieri, J.N. (1996). *Reason to read: Thinking strategies for life through learning.* Menlo Park, CA: Innovative Learning.

Block, C.C., & Mangieri, J.N. (2002). Recreational reading: 20 years later. *The Reading Teacher, 55*(6), 572–581.

Block, C.C., & Pressley, M. (2007). Best practices in teaching comprehension. In L.B. Gambrell, L.M. Morrow, & M. Pressley (Eds.), *Best practices in literacy instruction* (3rd ed., pp. 220–242). New York: Guilford.

Boraks, N., Hoffman, A., & Bauer, D. (1997). Children's book preferences: Patterns, particulars, and possible implications. *Journal of Reading, 18*(4), 309–341.

Bowker, R.R. (2000). *Bowker annual: Library and trade almanac.* New Providence, NJ: Author.

Brassell, D. (1999). Creating a culturally sensitive classroom library. *The Reading Teacher, 52*(6), 651–653.

Brenner, D., Tompkins, R., & Riley, M. (2007, November). *If I follow the teacher's manual, isn't that enough? Analyzing opportunity to read afforded by three core programs.* Paper presented at the 57th National Reading Conference, Austin, TX.

Buly, M.R. (2006). Independent reading. In M.E. Mooney & T.A. Young (Eds.), *Caught in the spell of writing and reading: Grade 3 and beyond* (pp. 123–154). Katonah, NY: Richard C. Owen.

California Department of Education. (2008). *The English-Language Arts content standards for California Public Schools (kindergarten through grade twelve).* Sacramento: California Department of Education.

Cameron, J., & Pierce, W.D. (1995). Reinforcement, reward, and intrinsic motivation: A meta-analysis. *Review of Educational Research, 64*(3), 363–423.

Caswell, L.J., & Duke, N.K. (1998). Non-narrative as a catalyst for literacy development. *Language Arts, 75*(2), 108–117.

Cervetti, G.N., Pearson, P.D., Bravo, M.A., & Barber, J. (2006). Reading and writing in the service of inquiry-based science. In R. Douglas, M.P. Klentschy, K. Worth, & W. Binder (Eds.), *Linking science and literacy in the K–8 classroom* (pp. 221–224). Arlington, VA: National Science Teachers Association.

Cooper, H., Charlton, K., Valentine, J.C., & Muhlenbruck, L. (2000). Making the most of summer school: A meta-analytic and narrative review. *Monographs of the Society for Research in Child Development, 65*(1), 1–118.

Cullinan, B.E. (2000). *Independent reading and school achievement.* Washington, DC: U.S. Department of Education.

Cunningham, A.E. (2006). Accounting for children's orthographic learning while reading text: Do children self-teach? *Journal of Experimental Child Psychology, 95*(1), 56–77.

Cunningham, A.E. (2005). Vocabulary growth through independent reading and reading aloud to children. In E.H. Hiebert & M.L. Kamil (Eds.), *Teaching and learning vocabulary: Bringing research to practice* (pp. 45–65). Mahwah, NJ: Erlbaum.

Cunningham, A.E., & Stanovich, K.E. (1991). Tracking the unique effects of print exposure in children: Associations with vocabulary, general knowledge, and spelling. *Journal of Educational Psychology, 83*(2), 264–274. doi:10.1037/0022-0663.83.2.264

Cunningham, A.E., & Stanovich, K.E. (1998). What reading does for the mind. *American Educator, 22*(1), 8–15.

Cunningham, P.M., & Allington, R.L. (2007). *Classrooms that work: They can all read and write* (4th ed.). Boston: Allyn & Bacon.

Daniels, H. (2002). *Literature circles: Voice and choice in book clubs and reading groups.* Portland, ME: Stenhouse.

Daniels, H. (2004). Building a classroom library. *Voices From the Middle, 11*(4), 44–46.

de Jong, P.F., & Share, D.L. (2007). Orthographic learning during oral and silent reading. *Scientific Studies of Reading, 11*(1), 55–71.

Divakaruni, C.B. (1997). *The mistress of spices.* New York: Anchor.

Doiron, R. (2003). Boy books, girls books: Should we re-organize our school library collections? *Teacher Librarian, 30*(3), 14–17.

Donovan, C.A., Smolkin, L.B., & Lomax, R.G. (2000). Beyond the independent-level text: Considering the reader-text match in first graders' self-selections during recreational reading. *Reading Psychology, 21*(4), 309–333. doi: 10.1080/02702710075 0061949

Dorris, M. (2006). Writers and readers: The book lives! *Booklist, 93*(6), 590–591.

Dreher, M.J., & Gray, J.L. (2009). Compare, contrast, comprehend: Using compare-contrast text structures with ELLs in K–3 classrooms. *The Reading Teacher, 63*(2), 132–141. doi:10.1598/RT.63.2.4

Duke, N.K. (2000). 3.6 minutes per day: The scarcity of informational texts in first grade. *Reading Research Quarterly, 35*(2), 202–224. doi:10.1598/RRQ.35.2.1

Duke, N.K. (2009, February). *Five things you can do to improve students' informational reading comprehension.* Presentation made at the annual conference of the Colorado Council of the International Reading Association, Denver, CO.

Durkin, D. (1966). *Children who read early: Two longitudinal studies.* New York: Teachers College Press.

Dymock, S. (2007). Comprehension strategy instruction: Teaching narrative text structure awareness. *The Reading Teacher, 61*(2), 161–167. doi:10.1598/RT.61.2.6

Elley, W.B., & Mangubhai, F. (1983). The impact of reading on second language learning. *Reading Research Quarterly, 19*(1), 53–67. doi:10.2307/747337

Fawson, P.C., & Moore, S.A. (1999). Reading incentive programs: Beliefs and practices. *Reading Psychology, 20*(4), 325–340. doi:10.1080/027027199278385

Felton, R.G., & Allen, R.F. (1990). Using visual materials as historical sources: A model for studying state and local history. *The Social Studies, 81*(2), 84–87.

Fielding, L.G., Wilson, P.T., & Anderson, R.C. (1986). A new focus on free reading: The role of trade books in reading instruction. In T.E. Raphael (Ed.), *The contexts of school-based literacy* (pp. 149–160). New York: Random House.

Fisher, D., Frey, N., & Lapp, D. (2008). Shared readings: Modeling comprehension, vocabulary, text structures, and text features for older readers. *The Reading Teacher, 61*(7), 548–556. doi:10.1598/RT.61.7.4

Fountas, I.C., & Pinnell, G.S. (2001). *Guiding readers and writers: Teaching comprehension, genre, and content literacy.* Portsmouth, NH: Heinemann.

Fractor, J.S., Woodruff, M.C., Martinez, M.G., & Teale, W.H. (1993). Let's not miss opportunities to promote voluntary reading: Classroom libraries in the elementary school. *The Reading Teacher, 46*(6), 476–484.

Gambrell, L.B. (2007). Reading: Does practice make perfect? *Reading Today, 24*(6), 16.

Gambrell, L.B. (2009). Creating opportunities to read more so that students read better. In E.H. Hiebert (Ed.), *Read more, read better* (pp. 251–266). New York: Guilford.

Gambrell, L.B., Codling, R.M., & Palmer, B.M. (1996). *Elementary students' motivation to read.* Athens, GA: National Reading Research Center.

Gambrell, L.B., & Mazzoni, S.A. (1999). Principles of best practice: Finding the common ground. In L.B. Gambrell, L.M. Morrow, S.B. Neuman, & M. Pressley (Eds.), *Best practices in literacy instruction* (pp. 11–21). New York: Guilford.

Gladwell, M. (2008). *Outliers: The story of success.* New York: Little, Brown.

Greenlaw, M.J., & Wielan, O.P. (1979). Reading interests revisited. *Language Arts, 56*(4), 32–34.

Guthrie, J.T. (2002). Preparing students for high-stakes testing in reading. In A.E. Farstrup & S.J. Samuels (Eds.), *What research has to say about reading instruction* (3rd ed., pp. 370–391). Newark, DE: International Reading Association.

Guthrie, J.T. (2004). Teaching for literacy engagement. *Journal of Literacy Research, 36*(1), 1–29. doi:10.1207/s15548430jlr3601_2

Guthrie, J.T., Anderson, E., Alao, S., & Rinehart, J. (1999). Influences of concept-oriented reading instruction on strategy use and conceptual learning from text. *The Elementary School Journal, 99*(4), 343–366. doi:10.1086/461929

Guthrie, J.T., & Greaney, V. (1991). Literacy acts. In R. Barr, M.L. Kamil, P.B. Mosenthal, & P.D. Pearson (Eds.), *Handbook of reading research* (Vol. 2, pp. 68–96). New York: Longman.

Guthrie, J.T., & McCann, A.D. (1996). Idea circles: Peer collaborations for conceptual learning. In L.B. Gambrell & J.F. Almasi (Eds.), *Lively discusssions! Fostering engaged reading* (pp. 87–105). Newark, DE: International Reading Association.

Guthrie, J.T., Schafer, W.D., Von Secker, C., & Alban, T. (2000). Contributions of integrated reading instruction and text resources to achievement and engagement in a statewide school improvement program. *The Journal of Educational Research, 93*(4), 211–226.

Guthrie, J.T., & Wigfield, A. (2000). Engagement and motivation in reading. In M.L. Kamil, P.B. Mosenthal, P.D. Pearson, & R. Barr (Eds.), *Handbook of reading research* (Vol. 3, pp. 403–422). Mahwah, NJ: Erlbaum.

Hadaway, N.L., Vardell, S.M., & Young, T.A. (2002). *Literature-based instruction with English language learners, K–12.* Boston: Allyn & Bacon.

Hadaway, N.L., Vardell, S.M., & Young, T.A. (2006). Language play, language work: Using poetry to develop oral language. In T.A. Young & N.L. Hadaway (Eds.), *Supporting the literacy development of English learners: Increasing success in all classrooms* (pp. 168–184). Newark, DE: International Reading Association.

Hancock, M.R. (2008). *A celebration of literature and response: Children, books, and teachers in K–8 classrooms.* Upper Saddle River, NJ: Merrill Prentice Hall.

Hanjian, L. (1985). *Are the interests of third grade students the same as the topics found in their classroom basal readers?* Union, NJ: Kean College of New Jersey.

Harkrader, M.A., & Moore, R. (1997). Literature preferences of fourth graders. *Reading Research and Instruction, 36*(4), 325–339.

Harvey, S., & Goudvis, A. (2007). *Strategies that work: Teaching comprehension for understanding and engagement.* Portland, ME: Stenhouse.

Hayes, D.P., & Ahrens, M. (1988). Vocabulary simplification for children: A special case of "motherese?" *Journal of Child Language, 15*(2), 395–410. doi:10.1017/S0305000900012411

Hearne, B. (2000). *Choosing books for children: A commonsense guide* (3rd ed.). Urbana, IL: University of Chicago Press.

Hepler, S.I., & Hickman, J. (1982). "The book was okay. I love you": Social aspects of response to literature. *Theory Into Practice, 21*(4), 278–283.

Herrick, V.E., & Jacobs, L.B. (1955). *Children and the language arts.* Englewood Cliffs, NJ: Prentice Hall.

Heyns, B. (1978). *Summer learning and the effects of schooling.* New York: Academic.

Hiebert, E.H., & Martin, L.A. (2009). Opportunity to read: A critical but neglected construct in reading instruction. In E.H. Hiebert (Ed.), *Reading more, reading better* (pp. 3–29). New York: Guilford.

Hiebert, E.H., Mervar, K.B., & Person, D.G. (1990). Children's selection of trade books in libraries and classrooms. *Language Arts, 67*(7), 758–763.

Hirsch, E.D., Jr. (2003). Reading comprehension requires knowledge—of words and the world. *American Educator, 27*(1), 10–29, 44–45.

Hirsch, E.D., Jr. (2006). The case for bringing content into the language arts block and for a knowledge-rich curriculum core for all children. *American Educator.* Retrieved April 4, 2006, from www.aft.org/pubs-reports/american_educator/issues/spring06/hirsch.htm

Hoffman, J.V., Roser, N.L., & Battle, J. (1993). Reading aloud in classrooms: From the modal toward the "model." *The Reading Teacher, 46*(6), 496–503.

International Reading Association. (1999). *Providing books and other print materials for classroom school libraries* (Position statement). Newark, DE: Author.

International Reading Association & National Council of Teachers of English. (1994). *Standards for the assessment of reading and writing.* Newark, DE; Urbana, IL: Authors.

Invernizzi, M., Rosemary, C., Juel, C., & Richards, H.C. (1997). At-risk readers and community volunteers: A 3-year perspective. *Journal of the Scientific Studies of Reading, 1*(3), 277–300.

Ivey, G., & Broaddus, K. (2001). "Just plain reading": A survey of what makes students want to read in middle school classrooms. *Reading Research Quarterly, 36*(4), 350–377.

Jennings, J., & Rentner, D.S. (2006). Ten big effects of the No Child Left Behind Act on public schools. *Phi Delta Kappan, 88*(2), 110–113.

Jobe, R., & Dayton-Sakari, M. (1999). *Reluctant readers: Connecting students and books for successful reading experiences.* Markham, ON: Pembroke.

Jones, J.A. (2006). Student-involved classroom libraries. *The Reading Teacher, 59*(6), 576–586. doi:10.1598/RT.59.6.7

Keene, E.O. (2008). *To understand: New horizons in reading comprehension.* Portsmouth, NH: Heinemann.

Keene, E.O., & Zimmermann, S. (2007). *Mosaic of thought: The power of comprehension strategy instruction.* Portsmouth, NH: Heinemann.

Kelley, M.J., & Clausen-Grace, N. (2006). R[5]: The sustained silent reading makeover that transformed readers. *The Reading Teacher, 60*(2), 148–156. doi:10.1598/RT.60.2.5

Kelley, M.J., & Clausen-Grace, N. (2007). *Comprehension shouldn't be silent: From strategy instruction to student independence.* Newark, DE: International Reading Association.

Kiefer, B.Z. (1988). Picture books as contexts for literary, aesthetic, and real world understandings. *Language Arts, 65*(3), 260–271.

Kiefer, B.Z., Hepler, S.I., & Hickman, J. (2006). *Charlotte Huck's children's literature.* New York: McGraw-Hill.

Kim, J. (2003, April). *Summer reading and the ethnic achievement gap.* Paper presented at the American Educational Research Association, Chicago, IL.

Kim, J. (2004). Summer reading and the ethnic achievement gap. *Journal of Education for Students Placed at Risk, 9*(2), 169–188.

Kim, J. (2006). The effects of a voluntary summer reading intervention on reading achievement: Results from a randomized field trial. *Educational Evaluation and Policy Analysis, 28*(4), 335–355.

Kletzien, S.B. (1998, December). *Information text or narrative text? Children's preferences revisited.* Paper presented at the National Reading Conference, Austin, TX.

Kletzien, S.B., & Dreher, M.J. (2004). *Informational text in K–3 classrooms helping children read and write.* Newark, DE: International Reading Association.

Kragler, S.D., & Nolley, C. (1996). Student choices: Book selection strategies of fourth graders. *Reading Horizons, 36*(4), 354–365.

Krashen, S.D. (1995). School libraries, public libraries, and the NAEP reading scores. *School Library Media Quarterly, 23*(4), 235–237.

Krashen, S.D. (1997). Bridging inequity with books. *Educational Leadership, 55*(4), 18–22.

Krashen, S.D. (1998). Every person a reader: An alternative to the California Task force report on reading. In C. Weaver (Ed.), *Reconsidering a balanced approach to reading* (pp. 425–452). Urbana, IL: National Council of Teachers of English.

Krashen, S.D. (2004). *The power of reading: Insights from the research* (2nd ed.). Portsmouth, NH: Heinemann.

Kuhn, M.R. (2000). *A comparative study of small group fluency instruction.* Unpublished doctoral dissertation, University of Georgia, Athens.

Kuhn, M.R. (2004). Helping students become accurate, expressive readers: Fluency instruction for small groups. *The Reading Teacher, 58*(4), 338–344. doi: 10.1598/RT .58.4.3.

Kuhn, M.R., & Schwanenflugel, P.J. (2009). Time, engagement, and support: Lessons from a 4-year fluency intervention. In E.H. Hiebert (Ed.), *Reading more, reading better* (pp. 141–160). New York: Guilford.

Kuhn, M.R., Schwanenflugel, P.J., Morris, R.D., Morrow, L.M., Woo, D.G., Meisinger, E.B., et al. (2006). Teaching children to become fluent and automatic readers. *Journal of Literacy Research, 38*(4), 357–387. doi:10.1207/s15548430jlr3804_1

Lacy, L. (1980). A Newbery honor book collection for elementary readers. *Top of the News, 37*(3), 297–301.

Lance, K.C., Welborn, L., & Hamilton-Pennell, C. (1993). *The impact of school library media centers on academic achievement.* Castle Rock, CO: Hi Willow Research and Pub

Lehman, B.A. (1991). Children's choices and critical acclaim: A united perspective for children's literature. *Reading Research and Instruction, 30*(3), 1–20.

Lukens, R.J. (2003). *A critical handbook of children's literature* (7th ed.). Boston: Allyn & Bacon.

Mandler, J.M. (1984). *Stories, scripts, and scenes: Aspects of schema theory.* Hillsdale, NJ: Erlbaum.

Manning, G.L., & Manning, M.A. (1984). What models of recreational reading make a difference? *Reading World, 23*(4), 266–273.

Marinak, B.A., & Gambrell, L.B. (2008). Intrinsic motivation and rewards: What sustains young children's engagement with text? *Literacy Research and Instruction, 47*(1), 9–26.

Martinez, M.G., Roser, N.L., Worthy, J., Strecker, S., & Gough, P. (1997). Classroom libraries and children's book selections: Redefining "access" in self-selected reading. In C.K. Kinzer, K.A. Hinchman, & D.J. Leu, Jr. (Eds.), *Inquiries in literacy theory and practice* (46th yearbook of the National Reading Conference, pp. 265–272). Chicago: National Reading Conference.

McCarthy, S.C. (2002). *Lay that trumpet in our hands.* New York: Bantam.

McQuillan, J. (1998). *The literacy crisis: False claims, real solutions.* Portsmouth, NH: Heinemann.

Mendoza, A. (1985). Reading to children: Their preferences. *The Reading Teacher, 38*(6), 522–527.

Miller, D. (2002). *Reading with meaning: Teaching comprehension in the primary grades.* Portland, ME: Stenhouse.

Miller, D. (2009). *The book whisperer: Awakening the inner reader in every child.* San Francisco: Jossey-Bass.

Miller, J. (2006). Shared writing. In M.E. Mooney & T.A. Young (Eds.), *Caught in the spell of writing and reading: Grade 3 and beyond* (pp. 61–76). Katonah, NY: Richard C. Owen.

Mitchell, D. (1998). Fifty alternatives to the book report. *English Journal, 87*(1), 92–95. doi:10.2307/822030

Monson, D.L., & Sebesta, S.L. (1991). Reading preferences. In J. Flood, J.M. Jensen, D. Lapp, & J.R. Squires (Eds.), *Handbook of research on teaching the English language arts* (pp. 664–673). New York: Macmillan.

Montabello, M. (1972). *Children's literature in the curriculum.* Dubuque, IA: Brown.

Mooney, M.E. (1990). *Reading to, with, and by children.* Katonah, NY: Richard C. Owen.

Mooney, M.E. (2001). *Text forms and features: A resource for intentional teaching.* Katonah, NY: Richard C. Owen.

Mooney, M.E. (2004). *A book is a present: Selecting text for intentional teaching.* Katonah, NY: Richard C. Owen.

Morrison, T.G., Jacobs, J.S., & Swinyard, W.R. (1999). Do teachers who read personally use recommended literacy practices in their classrooms? *Reading Research and Instruction, 38*(2), 81–100.

Morrow, L.M. (1983). Home and school correlates of early interest in literature. *The Journal of Educational Research, 76*(4), 221–230.

Morrow, L.M. (1992). The impact of a literature-based program on literacy achievement, use of literature, and attitudes of children from minority backgrounds. *Reading Research Quarterly, 27*(3), 250-275.

Morrow, L.M. (1993). *Literacy development in the early years: Helping children read and write* (2nd ed.). Boston: Allyn & Bacon.

Morrow, L.M. (2003). Motivating lifelong voluntary readers. In J. Flood, D. Lapp, J.R. Squire, & J.M. Jensen (Eds.), *Handbook of research on teaching the English language arts* (2nd ed., pp. 857–867). Mahwah, NJ: Erlbaum.

Morrow, L.M., Tracey, D.H., & Maxwell, C.M. (1995). *A survey of family literacy in the United States.* Newark, DE: International Reading Association.

Morrow, L.M., & Young, J. (1997). Parent, teacher, and child participation in a collaborative family literacy program: The effects of attitude, motivation, and literacy achievement. *Journal of Educational Psychology, 89*(4), 736–742.

Moss, B. (2008). The information text gap: The mismatch between non-narrative text types in basal readers and 2009 NAEP recommended guidelines. *Journal of Literacy Research, 40*(2), 201–219.

Moss, B., & Hendershot, J. (2002). Exploring sixth graders' selection of nonfiction trade books. *The Reading Teacher, 56*(1), 6–17.

Moss, G., & McDonald, J.W. (2004). The borrowers: Library records as unobtrusive measures of children's reading preferences. *Journal of Research in Reading, 27*(4), 401–412. doi: 10.1111/j.1467-9817.2004.00242.x.

Mullis, I.V.S., Campbell, J.R., & Farstrup, A.E. (1993). *NAEP 1992: Reading report card for the nation and the states.* Washington, DC: U.S. Department of Education.

Nagy, W.E., & Anderson, R.C. (1984). How many words are there in printed school English? *Reading Research Quarterly, 19*(3), 304–330. doi:10.2307/747823

National Center for Education Statistics. (2001). Progress in International Reading Literacy Study. Retrieved January 23, 2006, from timss.bc.edu/pirls2006/index.html

National Institute of Child Health and Human Development. (2000). *Report of the National Reading Panel. Teaching children to read: An evidence-based assessment of the scientific research literature on reading and its implications for reading instruction* (NIH Publication No. 00-4769). Washington, DC: U.S. Government Printing Office.

Nelson, K. (1986). *Event knowledge: Structure and function in development.* Hillsdale, NJ: Erlbaum.

Neuman, S.B. (1999). Books make a difference: A study of access to literacy. *Reading Research Quarterly, 34*(3), 286–311.

Neuman, S.B., & Celano, D. (2001). Access to print in low-income and middle-income communities: An ecological study. *Reading Research Quarterly, 36*(1), 8–26.

Noyes, D. (2000). *Developing the disposition to be a reader: The educator's role.* Retrieved January 20, 2010, from ceep.crc.uiuc.edu/pubs/katzsym/noyes.pdf.

Nystrand, M. (2006). Research on the role of classroom discourse as it affects reading comprehension. *Research in the Teaching of English, 40*(4), 392–412.

Oczkus, L.D. (2004). *Super six comprehension strategies: 35 lessons and more for reading success.* Norwood, MA: Christopher-Gordon.

Odean, C. (1997). *Great books for girls: More than 600 books to inspire today's girls and tomorrow's women.* New York: Ballantine.

Odean, C. (1998). *Great books for boys: More than 600 books for boys 2 to 14.* New York: Ballantine.

Ogle, D.M. (1986). K-W-L: A teaching model that develops active reading of expository text. *The Reading Teacher, 39*(6), 563–570.

Padak, N., & Rasinski, T. (2003). Family literacy programs: Who benefits? Retrieved May 18, 2008, from literacy.kent.edu/Oasis/Pubs/WhoBenefits2003.pdf

Palincsar, A., & Duke, N.K. (2004). The role of text and text-reader interactions in young children's reading development and achievement. *The Elementary School Journal, 105*(2), 183–197.

Palumbo, T.J., & Willcutt, J.R. (2007). Perspectives on fluency: English-language learners and students with dyslexia. In S.J. Samuels & A.E. Farstrup (Eds.), *What research has to say about fluency instruction* (pp. 159–178). Newark, DE: International Reading Association.

Paulsen, G. (2007). *About Gary Paulsen.* Retrieved July 17, 2007, from www.random house.com/kids/catalog/author.pperl?authorid=23384&view=sml_sptlght

Pearson, P.D. (2005, October). *Facilitating comprehension.* Presentation made to the Delaware Valley Reading Association, Springfield, PA. Retrieved March 16, 2010, from www.ciera.org/library/presos/2001/2001MRACIERA/pdp/01mrapdp.pdf

Pearson, P.D., & Gallagher, M.C. (1983). The instruction of reading comprehension. *Contemporary Educational Psychology, 8*(3), 317–344. doi:10.1016/0361-476X(83)90019-X

Perle, M., Moran, R., Lutkus, A.D., & Tirre, W. (2005). *NAEP 2004 trends in academic progress: Three decades of student performance in reading and mathematics.* Washington, DC: National Center for Education Statistics.

Pieronek, F.T. (1985). Do basal readers reflect the interests of intermediate students? *The Reading Teacher, 33*(4), 408–412.

Pikulski, J.J. (2007). Fluency: A developmental and language perspective. In S.J. Samuels & A.E. Farstrup (Eds.), *What research has to say about fluency instruction* (pp. 70–93). Newark, DE: International Reading Association.

Pinnell, G.S., & Jaggar, A.M. (2003). Oral language: Speaking and listening in elementary classrooms. In J. Flood, D. Lapp, J. Squire, & J. Jensen (Eds.), *Handbook of research on teaching the English language arts* (2nd ed., pp. 881–913). Mahwah, NJ: Erlbaum.

Pressley, M. (2002). *Reading instruction that works: The case for balanced teaching.* New York: Guilford.

Purves, A.C., & Monson, D.L. (1984). *Experiencing children's literature.* New York: Scott Foresman.

Ramos, F., & Krashen, S.D. (1998). The impact of one trip to the public library: Making books available may be the best incentive for reading. *The Reading Teacher, 51*(7), 614–615.

RAND Reading Study Group. (2002). *Reading for understanding: Toward an R&D program in reading comprehension.* Santa Monica, CA: RAND.

Ravitch, D., & Finn, C.E. (1987). *What do our 17 year olds know?* New York: HarperCollins.

Reutzel, D.R., & Fawson, P.C. (2002). *Your classroom library: Ways to give it more teaching power.* New York: Scholastic.

Reutzel, D.R., Fawson, P.C., & Smith, J.A. (2008). Reconsidering silent sustained reading: An exploratory study of scaffolded silent reading. *The Journal of Educational Research, 102*(1), 37–50. doi:10.3200/JOER.102.1.37-50

Reutzel, D.R., & Gali, K. (1998). The art of children's book selection: A labyrinth unexplored. *Reading Psychology, 19*(1), 3–50. doi:10.1080/0270271980190101

Reutzel, D.R., & Hollingsworth, P.M. (1991). Reading time in school: Effect on fourth graders' performance on a criterion-referenced comprehension test. *The Journal of Educational Research, 84*(3), 170–176.

Reutzel, D.R., Jones, C.D., Fawson, P.C., & Smith, J.A. (2008). Scaffolded silent reading: A complement to guided repeated oral reading that works! *The Reading Teacher, 62*(3), 194–207. doi:10.1598/RT.62.3.2

Rice, D.C., Dudley, A.P., & Williams, C.S. (2001). How do you choose science trade books? *Science and Children, 38*(6), 18–22.

Rinehart, S.D., Gerlach, J.M., Wisell, D.L., & Welker, W.A. (1998). Would I like to read this book? Eighth graders' use of book cover clues to help choose recreational reading. *Reading Research and Instruction, 37*(4), 263–280.

Rodriguez-Brown, F.V., Li, R.F., & Albon, J. (1999). Hispanic parents' awareness and use of literacy-rich environments at home and in the community. *Education and Urban Society, 32*(1), 41–58.

Ross, C.S., McKechnie, L., & Rothbauer, P.M. (2006). *Reading matters: What the research reveals about reading, libraries, and community.* Westport, CT: Libraries Unlimited.

Routman, R. (1999). *Conversations: Strategies for teaching, learning, and evaluating.* Portsmouth, NH: Heinemann.

Routman, R. (2003). *Reading essentials: The specifics you need to teach reading well.* Portsmouth, NH: Heinemann.

Samuels, S.J., & Wu, Y.-C. (2003). How the amount of time spend on independent reading affects reading achievement: A response to the National Reading Panel. Retrieved May 1, 2007, from www.tc.umn.edu/~samue001/web%20pdf/manuscript%20277-04.pdf

Saul, E.W. (2006). *Crossing borders: In literacy and science instruction.* Newark, DE: International Reading Association.

Schiefele, U. (1991). Interest, learning, and motivation. *Educational Psychologist, 26*(3–4), 299–324.

Segel, E., & Friedberg, J.B. (1991). Widening the circle: The beginning with books model. *The Horn Book Magazine, 67*(2), 186–189.

Share, D.L. (1999). Phonological recoding and orthographic learning: A direct test of the self-teaching hypothesis. *Journal of Experimental Child Psychology, 72*(2), 95–129.

Short, K.G., & Pierce, K.M. (1990). *Talking about books: Creating literate communities.* Portsmouth, NH: Heinemann.

Sinclair-Tarr, S., & Tarr, W. (2007). Using large-scale assessments to evaluate the effectiveness of school library programs in California. *Phi Delta Kappan, 88*(9), 710–712.

Smolkin, L.B., & Donovan, C.A. (2000). *The contexts of comprehension: Information book read alouds and comprehension acquisition* (CIERA Rep. No. #2-009). Ann Arbor, MI: Center for the Improvement of Early Reading Achievement.

Snow, C.E., Barnes, W.S., Chandler, J., Goodman, I.F., & Hemphill, L. (1991). *Unfulfilled expectations: Home and school influences on literacy.* Cambridge, MA: Harvard University Press.

Stahl, S.A. (2004). What do we know about fluency? Findings of the National Reading Panel. In P.D. McCardle & V. Chhabra (Eds.), *The voice of evidence in reading research* (pp. 187–211). Baltimore: Paul H. Brookes.

Stahl, S.A., & Heuback, K.M. (2005). Fluency-oriented reading instruction. *Journal of Literacy Research, 37*(1), 25–60.

Stanovich, K.E. (1986). Matthew effects in reading: Some consequences of individual differences in the acquisition of literacy. *Reading Research Quarterly, 21*(4), 360–407. doi:10.1598/RRQ.21.4.1

Stanovich, K.E., & Cunningham, A.E. (1993). Where does knowledge come from? Specific associations between print exposure and information acquisition. *Journal of Educational Psychology, 85*(2), 211–230. doi:10.1037/0022-0663.85.2.211

Stead, T. (2002). *Is that a fact? Teaching nonfiction writing K–3.* Portland, ME: Stenhouse.

Stead, T. (2009). *Good choice! Supporting independent reading and response K–6.* Portland, ME: Stenhouse.

Taberski, S. (2000). *On solid ground: Strategies for teaching reading K–3.* Portsmouth, NH: Heinemann.

Tabors, P.O., Snow, C.E., & Dickinson, D.K. (2001). Homes and schools together: Supporting language and literacy development. In D.K. Dickinson & P.O. Tabors (Eds.), *Beginning literacy with language: Young children learning at home and school* (pp. 313–334). Baltimore: Paul H. Brookes.

Taylor, B.M., Frye, B.J., & Maruyama, G.M. (1990). Time spent reading and reading growth. *American Educational Research Journal, 27*(2), 351–362.

Thomas, K.J., & Moorman, G.B. (1983). *Designing reading programs.* Dubuque, IA: Kendall/Hunt.

Thompson, L. (2005). *Guided reading: Years 5 to 8.* Wellington, NZ: Learning Media.

Tunnell, M.O., & Jacobs, J.S. (2008). *Children's literature, briefly* (4th ed.). Upper Saddle River, NJ: Merrill.

University of the State of New York and the State Education Department. (n.d.). The English language arts resource guide. Retrieved January 20, 2010, from www.emsc .nysed.gov/ciai/ela/pub/ccela.pdf

Vacca, R.T., & Vacca, J.L. (2008). *Content area reading: Literacy and learning across the curriculum* (9th ed.). New York: Pearson.

Vardell, S.M., Hadaway, N.L., & Young, T.A. (2002). Choosing and sharing poetry with ESL students. *Book Links, 11*(5), 51–56.

Wasik, B.H. (2004). *Handbook on family literacy.* Mahwah, NJ: Erlbaum.

Whitehead, N. (2004). The effects of increased access to books on student reading using the public library. *Reading Improvement, 41*(3), 165.

Wilhelm, J.D., Baker, T.N., & Dube, J. (2001). *Strategic reading: Guiding students to lifelong literacy, 6–12.* Portsmouth, NH: Heinemann.

Wiesendanger, K.D. (1982). Sustained silent reading: Its effect on comprehension and word recognition skills when implemented in a university summer reading clinic. *The Reading Professor, 8,* 33–37.

Worthy, J. (1996). Removing barriers to voluntary reading: The role of school and classroom libraries. *Language Arts, 73*(7), 483–492.

Worthy, J., Broaddus, K., & Ivey, G. (2001). *Pathways to independence: Reading, writing, and learning in grades 3–8.* New York: Guilford.

Worthy, J., Moorman, M., & Turner, M. (1999). What Johnny likes to read is hard to find in school. *Reading Research Quarterly, 34*(1), 12–27. doi:10.1598/RRQ.34.1.2

Wu, Y.C., & Samuels, S.J. (2004, May). *How the amount of time spent on independent reading affections reading achievement: A response to the National Reading Panel.* Paper presented at the 49th Annual Convention of the International Reading Association, Reno, NV.

Yoon, J.-C. (2002). Three decades of sustained silent reading: A meta-analytic review of the effects of SSR on attitude toward reading. *Reading Improvement, 39*(4), 186–195.

Young, C., & Rasinski, T.V. (2009). Implementing readers theatre as an approach to classroom fluency instruction. *The Reading Teacher, 63*(1), 4–13. doi:10.1598/RT.63 .1.1

Young, T.A. (2006a). Reading to students. In M.E. Mooney & T.A. Young (Eds.), *Caught in the spell of writing and reading: Grade 3 and beyond* (pp. 3–19). Katonah, NY: Richard C. Owens.

Young, T.A. (2006b). Weaving the magic together: Threads of student success and engagement. In M.E. Mooney & T.A. Young (Eds.), *Caught in the spell of writing and reading: Grade 3 and beyond* (pp. 175–189). Katonah, NY: Richard C. Owens.

Young, T.A., & Moss, B. (2006). Nonfiction in the classroom library: A literacy necessity. *Childhood Education, 82*(4), 207–213.

Young, T.A., & Vardell, S.M. (1993). Weaving Readers Theatre and nonfiction into the curriculum. *The Reading Teacher, 46*(5), 396–406.

CHILDREN'S LITERATURE CITED

Adkins, J. (2004). *What if you met a pirate? An historical voyage of seafaring speculation.* New York: Roaring Brook.

Allsburg, C.V. (1984). *The mysteries of Harris Burdick.* Boston: Houghton Mifflin.

Anderson, L.H. (2008). *Chains.* New York: Simon & Schuster.

Aston, D.H., & Long, S. (2006). *An egg is quiet.* New York: Chronicle.

Balliett, B. (2004). *Chasing Vermeer.* New York: Scholastic.

Bartoletti, S.C. (1996). *Growing up in coal country.* Boston: Houghton Mifflin.

Berger, M. (1995). *A whale is not a fish and other animal mix-ups.* New York: Scholastic.

Bishop, N. (2007). *Spiders.* New York: Scholastic.

Bolden, T. (2005). *Maritcha: A nineteenth century American girl.* New York: Abrams.

Bridges, R. (1999). *Through my eyes.* New York: Scholastic.

Broach, E. (2008). *Masterpiece.* New York: Henry Holt.

Bunting, E. (1989). *The Wednesday surprise.* New York: Clarion.

Bunting, E. (1998). *Going home.* New York: HarperCollins.

Burleigh, R. (1998). *Home run: The story of Babe Ruth.* San Diego, CA: Silver Whistle.

Burleigh, R. (2003). *Amelia Earhart: Free in the skies.* New York: Sandpiper.

Burns, M. (2008). *The greedy triangle.* New York: Scholastic.

Byrd, R. (2003). *Leonardo: Beautiful dreamer.* New York: Dutton.

Carle, E. (1999). *Dragons, dragons and other creatures that never were.* New York: HarperCollins.

Carle, E. (2002). *"Slowly, slowly, slowly," said the sloth.* New York: Philomel.

Carle, E. (2004). *Mister Seahorse.* New York: Philomel.

Choldenko, G. (2004). *Al Capone does my shirts.* New York: Putnam.

Codell, E.R. (2003). *Sahara special.* New York: Hyperion.

Colfer, E., & Donkin, A. (2007). *Artemis Fowl: The graphic novel.* New York: Hyperion.

Creech, S. (2001). *Love that dog.* New York: Cotler.

Criswell, P.K. (2006). *Friends: Making them and keeping them.* New York: American Girl.

Cronin, D. (2000). *Click, clack, moo: Cows that type.* New York: Simon & Schuster.

Curtis, C.P. (1995). *The Watsons go to Birmingham—1963.* New York: Delacorte.

D'Aluisio, F. (2008). *What the world eats.* New York: Tricycle.

d'Aulaire, I., & d'Aulaire, E.P. (2008). *Abraham Lincoln.* New Rochelle, NY: Spoken Arts.

Dahl, R. (2002). *Fantastic Mr. Fox.* New York: Random House.

Deem, J.M. (2005). *Bodies from the ash: Life and death in ancient Pompeii.* New York: Houghton Mifflin.

DePino, C. (2004). *Blue cheese breath and stinky feet: How to deal with bullies.* New York: Magination.

Dewey, J.O. (2000). *Rattlesnake dance: True tales, mysteries, and rattlesnake ceremonies.* New York: Boyds Mills.

DiCamillo, K. (2001). *Because of Winn-Dixie.* New York: Candlewick.

DiCamillo, K. (2004). *The tale of Despereaux: Being the story of a mouse, a princess, some soup, and a spool of thread.* New York: Scholastic.

Dotlich, R.K. (2001). *When riddles come rumbling: Poems to ponder.* Honesdale, PA: Wordsong/Boyds Mills.

Durant, A. (2006). *Burger boy.* New York: Clarion.

Eisner, W. (2003). *The princess and the frog.* New York: Nantier Beall Minoustchine.

Evanier, M., Bachs, R.F., & Fernandez, R. (2004). *Shrek.* Milwaukie, WI: Dark Horse.

Fleischman, P. (2000). *Big talk: Poems for four voices.* New York: Candlewick.

Foster, J. (2007). *How to be the best at everything: The girls' book: .* New York: Scholastic.

Fox, M. (1996). *Feathers and fools.* San Diego, CA: Harcourt.

Funke, C.C. (2003). *Inkheart.* New York: Chicken House/Scholastic.

Gardiner, J.R. (1980). *Stone Fox.* New York: HarperCollins.

Gardiner, J.R. (1980). *Stone Fox.* New York: Crowell.

Gibbons, G. (2007). *Snakes.* New York: Holiday House.

Gownley, J. (2009). *Amelia Rules! The whole world's crazy.* New York: Atheneum.

Greenberg, J. & Jordan, S. (2002). *Action Jackson.* Brookfield, CO: Roaring Brook.

Gutman, B. (2001). *Becoming best friends with your iguana, snake, or turtle.* New York: Millbrook.

Hawkins, C., & Hawkins, J. (2005). *Fairytale news.* Cambridge, MA: Walker.

Hayes, G. (2008). *Benny and Penny: Just pretend.* New York: Little Lit Library.

Heard, G. (1992). *Creatures of earth, sea, and sky: Animal poems.* Honesdale, PA: Wordsong/Boyds Mills Press.

Henkes, K. (1993). *Owen.* New York: Greenwillow.

Henkes, K. (1996). *Lilly's purple plastic purse.* New York: Greenwillow.

Henkes, K. (2004). *Kitten's first full moon.* New York: Greenwillow.

Holm, J.L. (2006). *Babymouse: Beach babe.* New York: Random House.

Holm, J.L. (2007). *Camp Babymouse.* New York: Random House.

Hopkins, L.B. (2002). *Spectacular science: A book of poems.* New York: Simon & Schuster.

Hopkinson, D. (2004). *Shutting out the sky: Life in the tenements of New York, 1880–1924.* New York: Orchard.

Hopkinson, D. (2008). *Abe Lincoln crosses a creek: A tall, thin tale (Introducing his forgotten frontier friend).* New York: Schwartz & Wade.

Howe, J. (2006). *Bunnicula meets Edgar Allan Crow.* New York: Atheneum.

Iggulden, C., & Iggulden, H. (2007). *The dangerous book for boys.* New York: HarperCollins.

Igus, T. (1998). *I see the rhythm.* San Francisco: Paw Prints.

Jeffrey, L.S. (2004). *Dogs: How to choose and care for a dog.* New York: Enslow.

Jenkins, S. (2002). *Life on earth: The story of evolution.* New York: Houghton Mifflin.

Jenkins, S., & Page, R. (2003). *What do you do with a tail like this?* Boston: Houghton Mifflin.

Johnson, J. (2009). *Animal tracks and signs.* Washington, DC: National Geographic.

Kasza, K. (2005). *My lucky day.* New York: Puffin.

Krensky, S. (2004). *There once was a very odd school and other lunch-box limericks.* New York: Dutton.

Krull, K. (2002). *Lives of the musicians: Good times, bad times (and what the neighbors thought).* San Diego, CA: Harcourt Brace Jovanovich.

Krull, K. (2008). *Hillary Rodham Clinton: Dreams taking flight.* New York: Simon & Schuster.

Krull, K. (2009). *Giants of science: Marie Curie.* New York: Puffin.

Kuskin, K. (2008). *The Philharmonic gets dressed.* New York: Paw Prints.

Lasky, K. (1994). *The librarian who measured the Earth.* New York: Little, Brown.

Lasky, K. (2001). *Surtsey: The newest place on Earth.* New York: Houghton Mifflin.

Lasky, K. (2003). *The man who made time travel*. New York: Melaine Kroups.

Lewis, J.P. (2007). *Scien-trickery: Riddles in science*. Orlando, FL: Voyager.

Livingston, M.C. (1993). *Abraham Lincoln: A man for all the people. A ballad*. New York: Holiday House.

Llewellyn, C. (2008). *Killer creatures*. New York: Kingfisher.

Lord, C. (2006). *Rules*. New York: Scholastic.

Lowry, L. (1989). *Number the stars*. Boston: Houghton Mifflin.

MacLachlan, P. (1985). *Sarah, plain and tall*. New York: HarperCollins.

Mannis, C.D. (2003). *The queen's progress: An Elizabethan alphabet*. New York: Viking.

Markle, S. (2004). *Great white sharks*. New York: Carolrhoda.

Mayer, M. (1994). *Baba Yaga and Vasilisa the Brave*. New York: Morrow.

McWhorter, D. (2005). *A dream of freedom: The Civil Rights movement from 1954 to 1958*. New York: Scholastic.

Mitchell, S. (2007). *The ugly duckling*. New York: Candlewick.

Moeri, L. (1994). *Save Queen of Sheba*. New York: Puffin.

Montgomery, S. (1999). *The snake scientist*. Boston: Houghton Mifflin.

Myers, W.D. (2006). *Jazz*. New York: Holiday House.

Napoli, D.J. (2010). *Mama Miti: Wangari Maathai and the treess of Kenya*. New York: Paula Wiseman/Simon & Schuster.

Naylor, P.R. (1991). *Shiloh*. New York: Atheneum.

Nelson, M. (2001). *Carver: A life in poems*. Asheville, NC: Front Street.

Neuschwander, C. (1999). *Sir Cumference and the new round table: A math adventure*. New York: Charlesbridge.

O'Dell, S. (1960). *Island of the blue dolphins*. Boston: Houghton Mifflin.

O'Neill, A. (2002). *The recess queen*. New York: Scholastic.

Osbourne, M.P. (1992–2010). *Magic Tree House*. New York: Random House.

Pappas, T. (1991). *Math talk: Mathematical ideas in poems for two voices*. New York: World Wide.

Parsons, A. (1990). *Amazing snakes*. New York: Knopf.

Patent, D.H. (2003). *Slinky, scaly, slithery snakes*. New York: Walker.

Paterson, K. (1977). *Bridge to Terabithia*. New York: HarperCollins.

Patron, S. (2006). *The higher power of Lucky*. New York: Atheneum/Richard Jackson.

Pilkey, D. (1996). *The paperboy*. New York: Scholastic.

Pilkey, D. (1997–2006). *Captain Underpants*. New York: Scholastic.

Polacco, P. (1994). *Pink and say*. New York: Philomel.

Prelutsky, J. (2004). *If not for the cat*. New York: Greenwillow.

Pringle, L.P. (2001). *Global warming: The threat of Earth's changing climate*. New York: Chronicle.

Rappaport, D. (2007). *Abe's honest words: The life of Abraham Lincoln*. New York: Hyperion.

Raschka, C. (2002). *John Coltrane's giant steps*. New York: Atheneum.

Reeder, T. (2005). *Poison dart frogs*. Washington, DC: National Geographic.

Repchuk, C. (1997). *The forgotten garden*. Minneapolis, MN: Millbrook.

Ride, S., & Okie, S. (1986). *To space and back*. New York: Lothrop Lee & Shepard.

Ringgold, F. (1991). *Tar beach*. New York: Crown.

Riordan, R. (2005). *The lightning thief: Percy Jackson and the Olympians, Book 1*. New York: Miramax.

Robinson, F. (2004). *Halloween crafts*. Berkeley Heights, NJ: Enslow.

Rowling, J.K. (1998). *Harry Potter and the sorcerer's stone*. New York: Scholastic.

Rubin, S.G. (2001). *The yellow house: Vincent van Gogh & Paul Gauguin side by side.* New York: Abrams.

Ryan, P.M. (2002). *When Marian sang: The true recital of Marian Anderson: The voice of a century.* New York: Scholastic.

Sachar, L. (1998). *Holes.* New York: Farrar, Straus and Giroux.

Sáenz, B.A. (1998). *A gift from Papá Diego/Un regalo de papá Diego.* New York: Cinco Puntos.

Schlitz, L.A. (2007). *Good masters! Sweet ladies! Voices from a medieval village.* New York: Candlewick.

Schwartz, D.M. (1998). *G is for Googol: A math alphabet book.* New York: Tricycle.

Scieszka, J. (1989). *The true story of the 3 little pigs!* New York: Viking.

Scieszka, J. (1995). *Math curse.* New York: Viking.

Scott, E. (1998). *Close encounters: Exploring the universe with the Hubble Space Telescope.* New York: Hyperion Books for Children.

Selznick, B. (2007). *The invention of Hugo Cabret.* New York: Scholastic.

Siegel, S.C. (2006). *To dance: A ballerina's graphic novel.* New York: Atheneum.

Sierra, J. (2006). *The secret science project that ate the school.* New York: Simon & Schuster.

Smith, C.R. (2007). *Twelve rounds to glory: The story of Muhammad Ali.* New York: Scholastic.

Snicket, L. (2002–2006) *A series of unfortunate events.* New York: HarperCollins.

Sohi, M.E. (1995). *Look what I did with a leaf!* New York: Walker.

Sohi, M.E. (2002). *Look what I did with a shell!* New York: Walker.

Soo, K. (2008). *Jellaby.* New York: Hyperion.

Sperry, A. (1940). *Call it courage.* New York: Macmillan.

Spinelli, J. (1993). *Maniac Magee.* New York: Collins.

St. George, J. (2000). *So you want to be president?* New York: Philomel.

Stanley, D. (1996). *Leonardo da Vinci.* New York: Morrow.

Stanley, D. (2000). *Michelangelo.* New York: HarperCollins.

Storrie, P.D. (2007). *Hercules: The 12 labors.* New York: Lerner.

Swope, S. (2001). *The Araboolies of Liberty Street.* New York: Farrar, Straus and Giroux.

Teague, M. (2004). *Detective LaRue: Letters from the investigation.* New York: Scholastic.

Thimmesh, C. (2000). *Girls think of everything: Stories of ingenious inventions by women.* Boston: Houghton Mifflin.

Thimmesh, C. (2006). *Team moon: How 400,000 people landed Apollo 11 on the moon.* Boston: Houghton Mifflin.

van der Rol, R., & Verhoeven, R. (1993). *Anne Frank: Beyond the diary.* New York: Viking.

van Gogh, V. (2005). *Vincent's colors.* San Francisco: Chronicle.

Vila, L. (2008). *Buidling Manhattan.* New York: Viking.

Waters, K., & Kendall, R. (2008). *Sarah Morton's day: A day in the life of a pilgrim girl.* New York: Scholastic.

White, E.B. (1952). *Charlotte's web.* New York: HarperCollins.

Wiesner, D. (2001). *The three pigs.* New York: Clarion.

Willems, M. (2003). *Don't let the pigeon drive the bus!* New York: Hyperion.

Willems, M. (2004). *Knuffle bunny: A cautionary tale.* New York: Hyperion.

Winter, J. (2007). *Diego.* New York: Knopf.

INDEX

Note: Page numbers followed by *f* and *t* indicate figures and tables, respectively.

wide reading and domain knowledge, 12–13, 125. *See also* independent reading
Wielan, O.P., 58
Wiesner, D., 50
Wigfield, A., 76
wikis, 114
Willcutt, J.R., 5
Willems, M., 51, 59
Williams, C.S., 128
Williams, L., 29
Wilson, P.T., 10*t*, 14, 17–18
Winfrey, Oprah, 1, 32
Winter, J., 126, 134*t*
Wisell, D.L., 58
Woodruff, M.C., 11*t*, 20, 35, 44*t*
Worthy, J., 10*t*, 53, 55–56

writing, responding to reading activities with, 110–112
writing centers in classroom libraries, 39
Wu, Y.-C., 9, 10*t*, 19–20

Y

Yoon, J.-C., 10*t*, 16
Young, C., 110
Young, J., 16
Young, T.A., 36, 53, 92, 93, 109, 110

Z

Zarnowski, Myra, 145–148
Zimmermann, S., 92, 93
Zmach, C., 29